PRAISE FOR **BECOMING A NONPROFIT PRO**

Tawnia Wise presents the principles in this book in a light-hearted yet practical way and can impact your nonprofit organization no matter what stage of development you're in—there is something for everyone! Even if you think you've already checked it off your list, revisit these areas with a frame of openness and long-term sustainability from the inside out. Tawnia and Wise Resource Development prioritize the teaching and implementation of these often-overlooked principles with their clients. They don't just provide services; they build relationships to educate and support their clients in becoming the best version of themselves, expanding our capacity to support our communities now and into the future.

—KATT ANDERSON
Director, Lightpath Health

It's been an honor knowing and witnessing the work of Tawnia Wise. When multiple funders stated that they recognized her work due to its quality and thoroughness, Wise Resource Development emerged as a major asset in helping the nonprofits in Southern Dallas. During my tenure at the State Fair of Texas as Vice President of Community Affairs, I was fortunate to fund her services to many agencies that, because of her assistance, have surpassed million-dollar budgets. Many of these agencies are led by people of color who did not have access to resources to grow their impact.

Tawnia's expertise is evident in her ability to have a massive client load, and more importantly, the results speak for themselves—so many agencies are thriving because of her knowledge. I'm excited about this book and the wisdom the reader will glean from her wealth of experience. It will enhance your toolkit for transformation!

—DR. FROSWA' BOOKER DREW
Founder, Reconciliation and Restoration Foundation
President, Soulstice Consultancy

Tawnia Wise is an experienced, thought-provoking leader who can share knowledge and experience in ways that are easy to understand and implement in real life. People who work for nonprofits are unique. They are driven to help make this world a better place. Having a tool, like *Become a Nonprofit Pro*, that can help our passionate professionals do this work is not only a necessary resource but valued and appreciated.

—CATHY BARKER
President and CEO, Jewish Family Service of Greater Dallas

Both new and seasoned fundraisers will find this to be a trusted reference for creating and executing a comprehensive revenue strategy. Tawnia utilizes real life scenarios from her career in fundraising to bring best practices to life in a realistic and simplified way that provides a reminder of the importance of the fundamentals in creating a diverse and sustainable fundraising portfolio.

—JAMIE WILLIAMS, MBA
Chief Executive Officer, It's Time Texas

Tawnia's book is a much needed source of knowledge, insight, and practical advice for the nonprofit community, based on her real world experience in supporting start ups and founder-led nonprofits. I've been privileged to work directly with her, as a colleague and advisor, and have seen firsthand the value she has brought to many of the nonprofits I work with, who are partners in the South Dallas Employment Project. I view her work as a major asset to the nonprofit community!

—WES JUREY
Managing Partner & Co-Founder, South Dallas Employment Project

Wise Resource Development knows all aspects of fundraising. They are strategic and thoughtful to their approach and tailor how they intersect with your organization based on your needs.

—MANDY SHREVE
Chief Administrative Officer, CitySquare

BECOME A
NONPROFIT PRO

TAWNIA WISE

BECOME A NONPROFIT PRO

9 COMMON PITFALLS AND HOW TO AVOID THEM

 Advantage | Books

Published by Advantage Books, Charleston, South Carolina.
An imprint of Advantage Media.

ADVANTAGE is a registered trademark, and the Advantage colophon is a trademark of Advantage Media Group, Inc.

Printed in the United States of America.

10 9 8 7 6 5 4 3 2 1

ISBN: 978-1-64225-901-8 (Paperback)
ISBN: 978-1-64225-900-1 (eBook)

Library of Congress Control Number: 2023908249

Book design by Analisa Smith.

This publication is designed to provide accurate and authoritative information in regard to the subject matter covered. It is sold with the understanding that the publisher is not engaged in rendering legal, accounting, or other professional services. If legal advice or other expert assistance is required, the services of a competent professional person should be sought.

Advantage Books is an imprint of Advantage Media Group. Advantage Media helps busy entrepreneurs, CEOs, and leaders write and publish a book to grow their business and become the authority in their field. Advantage authors comprise an exclusive community of industry professionals, idea-makers, and thought leaders. For more information go to **advantagemedia.com.**

This book is dedicated to my kids, Cole and Carmyn, for inspiring and pushing me to do the work to become my best self and for sacrificing, as kids of a single mom sometimes do, for a career that fuels our family.

CONTENTS

ACKNOWLEDGMENTS

To Advantage Media | Forbes Books, thank you for seeing that I had this book in me and partnering with me to bring it to the world. A special thanks to Caroline Moore for the pep talks and accountability that brought this to the finish line.

To Heather Quinn, Vanessa Delgado, Alex Hoenich, Heather Newell, Brittney Bannon, Rachel Assi, Emily Guthrie, Melanie Carroll, Pam Gill, Aimee Sheahan, Benjamin Bracken, Sommer Neff, Jeremy Gregg, Emily Cooke, Suzanne Smith, Jamie Williams, Amy Stewart, Jill Scigliano, Carmyn Wise, and Katt Anderson for providing insights, feedback, and influence that helped shape the book so that I could feel confident that it would serve as a valuable resource to the nonprofit sector.

To Jeff Meddaugh, my closest, dearest friend and the most talented copyeditor in the world, I could not have written this book without you. Thank you for the hours that you spent spinning my words into a better version without losing my voice.

To Heather Quinn, the first partner I have ever truly had in my life, you have elevated not just this book but WISE. It is such an amazing blessing to share a vision with someone who is as talented, dedicated, and insightful as you.

To Dr. Froswa Booker-Drew, Gabriela Norton, and the anonymous funder representatives (you know who you are), thank you for allowing me to give space to your insights so that others can learn from your wisdom.

To John Paine, thank you for taking me on as a coaching client when I was trying to figure out how to fix the things that seemed broken at WISE and for (with great kindness) helping me learn that what I really needed to focus on was my own mindset. And off we went on a journey of supportive self-work, during which you were the never-ending bringer of so many of the aha moments that have transformed my life and WISE.

To Terri Maxwell, founder of ShiftCo and my brilliant business coach. You taught me about how to turn effective quality services into a successful business with your expertise, encouragement, and transformative tools, processes, strategy, and mindset shifts. What you do to inspire and grow conscious business leaders is changing lives and creating ripples of impact throughout the world.

To Trey Bize, you didn't know it at the time, but that phone call you made when you saw the write-up about my golf tournament in the newspaper became a cautionary tale that has been told and retold for years. Thank you for the lesson you taught me about the foolishness of withholding an opportunity.

To all the past, current, and future WISE clients, I am beyond thankful for the privilege of working with you and for all that I have learned through the experiences—much of it has influenced this book and will continue to make WISE a better and more effective consultancy.

To those organizations and people named explicitly or anonymously in the book, I am beyond thankful for the lessons learned. Every experience made me a more effective consultant with the opportunity to pay those lessons forward—hopefully, the ripple effect will be an endless relay of doing better.

To Carmyn Wise and Heather Quinn, the only two people (other than the editors) who had a chance to read this book from cover to cover in its rough draft, thank you for your patience, support, and feedback.

INTRODUCTION

When approached with the idea to write a book about my work with nonprofits, I became excited at the opportunity to put the most common advice that I give into a format that can reach more people and have a broader impact than what I can achieve personally as a consultant and what Wise Resource Development (WISE) can as a consultancy.

Before starting WISE in 2014, I spent my career in nonprofits. I was able to gain experience at nonprofits of different sizes, levels of sophistication, and stages of the organizational life cycle. I leveraged that experience to build a consultancy that I love. I wake up on most days knowing I am lucky that I get to do this work every day.

Because every consultant at WISE has worked in-house in nonprofits and has fundraising and leadership experience, WISE specializes in working with founder-led organizations. We know what it is like to be overworked and underresourced. We understand fundraising best practices, how nonprofits operate, and how to design programs.

While the book is written with a target audience of nonprofit founders, executive directors, board members, and other nonprofit leaders at organizations that are in the start-up phase, my hope is that anyone who serves a nonprofit that they love in some capacity will gain some value from *Become a Nonprofit Pro*.

I always like to be clear that the start-up phase is not time dependent for nonprofits. It is behavioral, and organizations can still be in a start-up phase into their thirtieth year of operation and beyond. The start-up phase is usually characterized as having a lack of formalized structures. It can be defined by the scrappy "Get it done on a shoestring" mindset that limits investment in strategy, planning, professionalism, structure, and growth.

If you picked up this book because you're thinking about forming a nonprofit, it will help you do a gut check on your intentions and prepare for a major undertaking. A word of caution if your goal is to save a failing for-profit business by transforming it into a nonprofit or to create a job for yourself: Just as a deteriorating company won't attract investors, an ineffective nonprofit won't convince funders to donate to their cause. To make either work, you must be financially solvent, forward-thinking, and business savvy.

And going into it, consider the major differences between a nonprofit and a for-profit. If you own a for-profit company, you make all the decisions. Profits are yours, and you can keep financial information private. If you lead a nonprofit, you report to a board of directors, and the company belongs to the public. The board makes the decisions, including major financial and strategy ones. Additionally, financials are not private. They are public documents and are used by potential donors to determine your financial competency and **compliance**.

If you are currently leading a nonprofit, this book is designed to help you take it to the next level. It is broken down into nine chapters, each a common pitfall that can have significant consequences on the health, sustainability, and effectiveness of a nonprofit. Since my background—and the WISE consultancy's expertise—is in fundraising, the book is written through the lens of fundraising and being competitive for donor investment.

In some cases, I refer to the WISE consultancy as "we," and there are some terms that I use interchangeably, including **development** and **fundraising**. I have included a glossary of terms at the back of the book for quick reference. Glossary words or terms are highlighted throughout the book.

In many cases the organizations referred to have been fictionalized. Names and minor details have been changed to protect identities. However, the scenarios described in examples, including the *Getting It WISE* (clients who "got it right" and serve as success stories) and *WISE Cautionary Tales* (I love a good cautionary tale—learn from others so you don't have to make the same mistakes) sections, are as close to my experience and recollection as possible.

For each chapter, refer to www.wiseresourcedevelopment.com for downloadable resources, tools, and templates.

Thank you for picking up this book and taking this journey with me. I'm here to help you improve your nonprofit in ways you might never have considered. Let's get to work!

CHAPTER 1

You Believe Fundraising Will Solve All Your Problems

The majority of people who engage the WISE consultancy are seeking fundraising support. As such, I think it is important to start this book by explaining how fundraising relates to the overall health and sustainability of a nonprofit. To do this, we'll talk through the basic structure of a functioning nonprofit utilizing the three-legged stool metaphor.

Three-Legged Stool: Your Mission Relies Equally on Programs, Operations, and Fundraising

A well-intentioned mission and strong fundraising efforts cannot compensate for programming and operational systems that are broken or not formally structured. That's why, when nonprofits come to us for fundraising strategy, we look at these systems holistically—oftentimes much to their surprise. Your organization, whether in its infancy or fifteenth year, needs to be operationally sound to be sustainable and fundable.

How do you build a stool that can withstand the weight of your mission? Each leg has a purpose that contributes to the overall strength of the stool. Let's see what this looks like.

Your Mission's Purpose is to Meet a Demonstrated Need

Your mission, or the seat of the stool, is your *why*.

If you aim to launch a new nonprofit, first understand the **community need**. This involves making sure you're not trying to fill the same gap other local nonprofits are. While I respect someone's personal calling to meet a need, it is essential to find the optimum way to plug in before launching a nonprofit. Currently, there are more than 1.5 million nonprofits registered with the Internal Revenue Service

(IRS) and fighting over the same $471.44 billion (which averages out to roughly $300,000 in donations given annually per nonprofit). Not only is it inefficient to duplicate services in a community, but a nonprofit also won't be viable over the long term if it can't be competitive for funding. Funders have started pushing organizations to merge for this very reason. Therefore, before starting a new nonprofit, research your nonprofit landscape.

If there is a true and clear need or gap in services, ask these questions:

- What makes you and your new nonprofit most qualified to meet that need?

- Do you have a relationship to the target market you aim to serve?

- Do you have access to funding sources?

Your answers will be some of your selling points to funders, especially when you don't yet have a track record of **community impact**.

GETTING IT WISE: DEMONSTRATE QUALIFICATIONS

One of our clients in the start-up phase provides pro bono legal services for youth and young adults imprisoned while they were minors. The founder launched the organization with compelling experience and statistical information that demonstrated how it is uniquely qualified to meet the needs of this population. The qualifications are based on the professional experience and credentials of the organization's leadership: *"No other organization combines **evidence-based best practices** in health, law, and criminology to impact those entering the justice system and those who have already been convicted."*

The client is also able to demonstrate that it has access to and deep knowledge about the population it is serving.

Your **value proposition** is what makes your organization unique and most qualified. If there is another nonprofit providing services similar to yours, you must—to be competitive for funding—be able to demonstrate what makes your organization unique by answering the following:

- Are you serving a different population or geographical area?

- Do you have a different approach or service model?

- What makes your service model better than existing options?

Your Program's Purpose Is to Demonstrate Impact

Programs are how your mission is fulfilled, and they must provide proof to funders that what you're doing has real impact. Funders want to fund demonstrated results or, for a new program, a well-thought-out plan to meet a specific need. When you make any kind of purchase, you want to know what you are investing in for your moneys—funders do too!

WISE PRO TIP: DESIGNING A NEW PROGRAM

When designing a new program, consider the following:

- Is there evidence-based research that you can use to develop your program?

- Are there other organizations or program models in other parts of the country that you could model your program after?

- Are they serving a similar population in a similar geographical area?

- What are they doing really well that you can reasonably replicate?

- Are they willing to serve as a consultant to support your program implementation?

We are often hired by nonprofits to implement a grant-writing strategy. But because doing so can reveal weaknesses in an organization's program model, sometimes our first step is to help them develop a formal program structure. This is so that we can talk about the programs in a way a funder will understand. This process is not uncommon, and we encourage you to embrace it, even if you have been implementing your program for decades. Many nonprofits evolve organically, and taking the time to reassess the health and structure of your program through the lens of a rigorous grant-application process will, in the end, make it stronger in impact and more sellable to funders.

In doing this work, it's important to think through every detail of the program and how it leads to the desired impact. Here we like to use a **logic model**, a common tool used by nonprofits to outline the inputs, activities, timelines, outputs, and outcomes associated with your program. Some funders ask for this. If the program is a crisis call center, for example, here are some potential questions a logic model will guide you through answering:

- Where will it be housed?

- What equipment is needed?

- Who will oversee it?

- What qualifications and training will the staff or **volunteers** need?

- What is the client experience from start to finish?

- How will impact or results be measured?

- What does success look like?

Funders have the right to know the results of their donation. These are usually referred to as impact or **outcome measures**. They are the **key performance indicators** (KPIs) of programmatic success. Unfortunately, many nonprofits do not track outcomes. Without being able to provide evidence of impact, how do you—and your funders—know you are successful in your mission?

We recommend that when determining how impact will be measured, your programs *and* fundraising staff should be involved. This is important because your fundraisers often have a better sense for what funders expect to see regarding metrics. And while you must walk the line of not adapting your programs to the whims of funders, you need their support to remain viable.

GETTING IT WISE: BE COMPETITIVE

A previous client of ours was implementing the Working Families Success Model, a nationally recognized and evidence-based model that moves individuals and families out of poverty through an approach that bundles basic needs and income supports, financial coaching, job skills training, and employment coaching. Having a solid understanding of this model and how organizations are implementing it and tracking its success, I pointed out the importance of tracking changes in an individual's FICO score, which, along with reflecting an individual's ability to get fair credit and carry a lower burden when it came to deposits for utilities and other services, could be used as an impact measurement. The program staff, however, was hesitant to factor this into their programming because they wouldn't be able to pull the scores without client consent. But when I explained that funders expect to see this type of outcome and that other organizations were able to track this metric, she was anxious to be competitive for funding and began tracking FICO scores.

Competition can be seen as an ugly word in the nonprofit world. But the reality is when you ask for a donation, you are vying for the same dollars many other nonprofits are after. The positive here is that when nonprofits are pushed to prove impact in similar ways, a **benchmark** is established. Still, if your outcomes don't meet that benchmark, it doesn't mean you no longer qualify for that funding. It might mean you have some explaining to do to make the funder understand your unique situation. For instance, does the population you serve have more barriers to success?

> Competition can be seen as an ugly word in the nonprofit world. But the reality is when you ask for a donation, you are vying for the same dollars many other nonprofits are after.

GETTING IT WISE: USE COMPARISON

When you are articulating the success of your programs, consider the difference between the status quo and the direct impact your organization makes. Comparison is an important consideration when measuring program success. For example, one client that helps returning citizens successfully transition from incarceration describes its outcomes in the following way:

> *Our character-based program model has produced industry-leading results with recidivism rates (return to prison) consistently below 9 percent (compared to the Texas three-year average of 21.4 percent), dropping to approximately 4 percent for those who live in transitional homes and graduate from our postrelease program.*

The client measures recidivism in the same way the state does so that it can compare its results. It has also identified recidivism data from other reentry programs for comparison.

Your Operations' Purpose is to Protect Your Mission

Operations refers to the procedures and systems a nonprofit uses to carry out day-to-day activities. Some common operational issues that we see involve financial accounting and human resources-related challenges—important organizational functions for nonprofits of any size.

A **sustainable** and accountable nonprofit must have adequate **financial systems** and operate with **financial transparency**. This means if there is not someone on staff with nonprofit accounting expertise, there must be a hired consultant or board member with this capability. We will review financial systems in chapter 2, but I want to touch on the importance of financial transparency here, as financial issues are one of the easiest ways to damage your operational leg. Too many times, I have witnessed the results of an **executive director** manipulating financial reports or presenting them in a way that downplays a negative financial position. Not only is this unethical, but it also puts the organization and the board members (who are **fiscally responsible** for the organization) at risk and inhibits their ability to do their job (ensuring the success and sustainability of the organization). Financial issues must be dealt with head on. They do not resolve themselves while in hiding.

Another common operational issue involves the lack of HR systems and expertise. Again, if you do not have this expertise on staff, get it through a consulting relationship or a board member. Implement a formal **performance management** process, and make sure that you know the applicable employment laws. Dealing with terminations can become a nightmare and consume valuable nonprofit resources if you make missteps that involve employment law.

A WISE CAUTIONARY TALE: PERFORMANCE MANAGEMENT SYSTEMS PROTECT YOUR MISSION

We had a client who terminated a supervisor when a race-related grievance was filed by a subordinate. There was some debate on whether this complaint was filed in earnest or in response to the supervisor addressing performance. This "he-said-she-said" situation was complicated by the fact there was no formal performance management system in place that would have protected all parties involved—

the supervisor, the subordinate, *and* the organization. While in this case, the grievance and the subsequent termination did not result in a lawsuit, it did result in significant damage to the culture of the organization and led to a complete turnover of the impacted department. Following this, the organization implemented a formal performance management system. Doing so not only better protects them from a potential future wrongful termination lawsuit, but it also clarifies expectations and creates accountability for staff.

Cultural issues are extremely common in nonprofits and require intentionality to mitigate, especially as your organization grows. Many nonprofits can be crippled by turf wars and siloed departments, all of which can ultimately damage the organization's efforts in fundraising, outreach, and programming.

One of our clients had such siloed marketing and fundraising departments that they were using different mailing lists. The marketing department was sending communications to a deceased donor, angering family members who were also active supporters of the organization. This lack of communication between departments will, at best, create inefficiencies and, at worst, devalue the organization's reputation and **brand**.

Utilize formal HR processes and procedures to promote the culture you desire within your nonprofit. Culture is driven by organizational leadership, both in setting and modeling clear expectations. We'll talk more about culture in chapter 7.

Your Fundraising's Purpose is to Sustain Community Impact

Fundraising financially fuels your programs and operations and must be sustainable with diversified revenue streams and robust individual giving.

There are three types of donors around which organizations build fundraising strategies: individuals, corporations, and institutional funders (grant-making entities). Individual giving comprises almost 68 percent of all giving in the United States, with foundation giving at 19 percent and corporate giving at 3 percent.[1] Year over year, individuals have proven to be the most reliable donors. This is why it is best practice for nonprofits to have strong individual donor **giving strategies**. We will discuss diversification of revenue streams in chapter 3.

There are many fundraising strategies that tap into giving from the three different types of donors, including grant writing, special events, annual appeals and campaigns, giving days, and **capital campaigns**. There are advantages and disadvantages to each of these, but having a mix of strategies with a focus on individual giving and unrestricted revenue is the key to building a strong fundraising leg. We will go into fundraising strategies in more detail in chapter 9.

Another important consideration when developing sustainable fundraising strategies is whether the gift is restricted. **Unrestricted revenue** means that the organization's leadership can decide how to spend those funds.

---

1   "Giving USA Limited Data Tableau Visualization: Giving USA,"
     givingusa.org (Giving USA, October 6, 2021), https://givingusa.org/
     giving-usa-limited-data-tableau-visualization/.

WISE PRO TIP: AVOID RESTRICTING YOUR ASK

Individual donors are much more likely to give unrestricted gifts than institutional donors. Still, in all asks, it is important not to unnecessarily restrict the gift. Remember this, especially when it comes to special appeals. Nonprofits can unwittingly restrict their gifts in an appeal by saying something like, "Your gift of $50 will provide a backpack for a student this fall."

What happens when you get more donations for backpacks than you need? Or what if you never intended to spend the $50 on backpacks, but you were trying to follow the best practice of helping donors understand the value of their gift? I hate to break it to you, but in the ask, you promised the donor how their gift would be spent. You restricted the gift to backpacks.

Instead of using "will," use "could" to provide the concept of what $50 *could* do. This way, you are giving yourself room to spend the money in a different way if the need arises.

Often, one or more of the legs of an organization's stool is structurally damaged. It can be hidden for a time but will eventually reveal itself—often when a stakeholder, like a funder, tries to sit upon the stool, and it collapses under their weight. Let's take a look at what happened with Holly's Haven.

A WISE CASE STUDY: HOLLY'S HAVEN

When we first started working with Holly's Haven, an organization that provides social and emotional learning (SEL) through out-of-school-time activities, it was a darling in the community. It was a small organization led by Becky, its cofounder and executive director, and four program staff. Becky was charismatic and well connected with area funders, so raising money was easy for Holly's Haven.

Becky hired us with visions of growth. She wanted to expand services into other low-income neighborhoods that had a clear need. As she explained it, her SEL programs were proven to work. After all, she had several stories of program alumni who went on to graduate from college and become successful professionals, breaking out of generations of poverty. She was sure that growing the program would get funders' support. Becky aimed to raise $500,000, which would allow Holly's Haven to secure larger space, hire staff, and double the number of youths served each year to five hundred. This growth campaign would conveniently take place during their ten-year anniversary.

When WISE takes on a growth or capital campaign project, we conduct a **fundraising assessment** as part of the **feasibility study** and planning process. This is to determine the campaign's viability and build a strategy that leverages the organization's unique assets as well as mitigates any threats to the campaign's success. The assessment of Holly's Haven revealed some weaknesses in their programs and operations.

During its first nine years of operation, Holly's Haven was well funded by grants. But that whole time, it stayed in start-up mode without systems and processes that would help it execute efficient, effective programs and fundraising activities. The organization never invested in a **constituent relationship management (CRM) system**, so student, partner, and donor data were tracked haphazardly in multiple Excel spreadsheets. Staff tracked the number of students served but didn't track changes in emotional resiliency or social or coping skills, so it was difficult for them to demonstrate community impact.

Holly's Haven was also stuck in a loop of constant turnover. Program staff were paid a low wage, and many of them were so inexperienced that it required Becky to spend significant *resources* to ramp them up. It would often take her at least six months to a year to get new staff members to a point where they could work independently, but by then, they would often take their new skills and leave for a better-paying job. This endless cycle of staff renewal was impacting the organization's sustainability and its ability to build structure that allowed for *strategic* growth. Becky was also not well paid, but she loved the work and the flexibility it provided while she worked on her master's degree.

Up until that point, the organization's small annual budget of $250,000 was covered by a handful of private family foundations who trusted and believed in Becky. The board of directors was chaired by the cofounder, Holly, and included five other members who were mostly there to support their friends. While they seemed excited about the growth campaign, they moaned at the mention of participating in fundraising efforts.

To prepare for the campaign, I met one-on-one with each of their top five major donors and asked them about their interest in supporting the organization's growth strategy. Each expressed concerns about whether the organization was ready for the level of growth outlined in the plan. Four of the five said they would support the campaign with an additional gift that would be above and beyond their annual gift. Only one of those would give a significantly higher amount than their annual gift. One also said they considered giving to another project instead in which the younger members of their family were more interested. Following these frank conversations, we estimated Holly's Haven could count on its closest donors for a total of $100,000—much less than its $500,000 goal. This was a disappointing blow to Becky.

In our work, we also conducted research to come up with a list of additional **grant funders** who might be interested in supporting the campaign. We met with several of these **prospects**. Unfortunately, they expressed reservations. They wanted to see Holly's Haven secure at least 50 percent of its fundraising goal first. They also preferred to see more individual donor support and a plan for how the growing operational budget would be funded after the campaign. Concern was expressed, too, about the level of growth Holly's Haven was aiming for, its **organizational readiness**, and its programmatic impact.

In analyzing its individual **donor base**, I uncovered more trouble. Most donors were not actively engaged with the organization. Holly's Haven had not been consistently communicating with them. There were no newsletters or other forms of regular communication.

Subsequently, I advised Becky that the organization's campaign goal should be no more than $250,000, as this was the most reasonable goal that could be achieved without cannibalizing the funding they needed to operate. This hit her hard.

Becky's time had come. She had finished her studies and graduated with dreams of launching her own social impact business. She announced she was leaving Holly's Haven. On her way out, Becky had two recommendations to board members: abandon the campaign and merge the organization with a larger one.

Seemingly relieved at the suggestion, the board agreed. This effort spanned more than two years and involved at least three failed merger attempts, leaving the organization without executive leadership, active fundraising efforts, or a stable staff. Holly's Haven saw turnover in all staffing positions, had several temporary executive directors, and went from being a darling of the funding community to barely surviving.

At this point, board members had a decision to make—shutter the organization or develop a comeback plan. When they returned for advice, we hoped to be part of their comeback story. We helped to place an interim staff person to answer phones and coordinate operations. From there, they were able to search for a new executive director, begin to strengthen their sustainability, and win back the trust and support of funders.

Holly's Haven lacked the operational infrastructure and demonstrated programmatic impact that would've allowed them to steward their donors in a meaningful way. The strength of the fundraising leg was a mirage. Outside of grant writing, the organization didn't have a fundraising strategy.

Funders talk to each other, and they know the signs of struggle. They won't keep investing in a floundering nonprofit—which is exactly what happened to Holly's Haven. It lost its status with grant funders. Its individual donor base was negligible, so it had no one to rely on when its dynamic leader left, and the lack of sustainable operational structure and demonstrable impact began to reveal itself.

Word to the WISE

A sustainable organization relies on the stability of all parts of the stool. Each needs to be effectively serving its purpose. The mission (seat) needs to be one that is meeting a demonstrated need. The operations leg needs to have effective systems that protect the mission. The programs leg needs to be demonstrating impact. And the fundraising leg needs to be sustaining mission impact. Take a moment to ask yourself if there is a weakness in the structure of your stool. Read on for some more tips that will help you fix it.

CHAPTER

2

PITFALL **2**

Your Financials Tell the Wrong Story

Now that you know how important financial systems are to the operations leg of your stool, let's explore that further.

Did you know that your financials tell a story? Funders look at several documents, including your organizational budget, **balance sheet**, statement of activities, IRS Form 990, and financial audit, to determine whether your nonprofit is worthy of investment. In this chapter, I'll walk through each of these documents and what they tell a funder about your organization.

Building a Budget that Tells a Story of Planning and Foresight

Unlike those of for-profit companies, the annual budgets of nonprofits are static, board-approved documents. The board approves the budget before the beginning of an organization's **fiscal year**. If an organization receives less funding than expected or its spending differs from what was projected, forecast budgets can be created throughout the year to reflect these changes so that progress toward a more realistic financial projection can be tracked. Using dynamic **financial management software** makes this process easier.

We often encounter organizations that do not have board-approved budgets. Without this invaluable guide, you are not ready to seek grant funding. Showing successful performance toward a board-approved budget (staying aligned with projected expenses or not **deficit** spending) reflects an organization's fiscal responsibility and sustainability. Potential grant funders want to see this minimum level of financial management as they decide whether to make an investment.

While not every organization develops its budget in the same manner, WISE recommends that it is based on realistic **revenue projections**. Sometimes, well-meaning nonprofits plug their ideal expenses into a budget and then develop their revenue projections based on the amount of money they want to spend. But for some, it becomes obvious after a review of their fundraising history that they don't have the track record of raising the amount of money on which they've based their expenses. In this case, deficit spending is not far behind.

If you have been operating for more than a year, your historical revenue data will help you determine realistic revenue goals, and we recommend doing this in the form of a **development plan**. This plan outlines exactly how the revenue goals attached to the budget will be achieved. We will talk about how to do this in chapter 9.

When you are trying to expand programs and have stretched revenue goals to accomplish that, or you are concerned that your revenue projections are lofty, we recommend creating a two-tier budget. The first tier is based on what you know you can raise the funds for. The second is your stretch budget of services you can provide if your plan to raise funds for the full budget is achieved.

In starting to build a budget, let's first dig into expenses. What does it really cost to operate your agency? Start with staffing. What was the cost of staffing last fiscal year, including wages, employment taxes, training, travel, and paid leave? Do you plan to provide any wage increases or hire additional staff in the coming year? What is your fixed overhead—rent, mortgage, vehicles, insurance, utilities? Include all fixed monthly or annual expenses.

Note that in-kind donations hit both as revenue and as an equal expense, so they show as a wash in the budget.

Does your organization require volunteers to function? If so, include the value of that in-kind volunteer labor. *In-kind donations* are often a large part of a small nonprofit's budget. Food, clothing, and gift card donations are all part of what it costs to run your organization—track them and include them in your budget. Note that in-kind donations hit both as revenue and as an equal expense, so they show as a wash in the budget. For example, if the executive director donates her time, the market rate value of that donated salary should be included in the budget as an expense and as an in-kind revenue donation.

The goal is to build a budget that fully reflects what it takes to operate your organization. The in-kind contributions of a volunteer-driven nonprofit could exceed $100,000. So now your $60,000 annual budget just turned into a $160,000 one. That difference will have a significant impact on how you ask for funding.

Let me explain. If you're going to ask for grant funding, two pieces of information will determine the amount of the ask. One is the size of your budget. The other is the funder's historical giving. Most funders are not going to fund more than 25 percent of your budget (savvy funders know that this puts your long-term sustainability at risk). If your expenses are $60,000, the most you can ask for is about $15,000 toward your budget. But if your true budget, including in-kind considerations, is $160,000, you'll be able to ask for about $40,000. This is particularly important if you hope to have that salary be paid in the future or you have a loss of in-kind support and need **philanthropic dollars** to cover the need.

Including this level of specificity tells the story that you are detail oriented, organized, and forward-thinking.

WISE PRO TIP: DO SCENARIO PLANNING DURING THE BUDGETING PROCESS

The COVID-19 pandemic made this a painful lesson for some. It showed what it takes for a nonprofit to survive, and it exposed the organizations that could not operate sustainably or demonstrate relevancy.

Nonprofits tend to undersell themselves. They don't want to ask for too much money and are often stuck in the mindset that nonprofits shouldn't be financially comfortable or dare request more than is needed to keep the lights on. That mindset limits growth and is not sustainable over the long term. The COVID-19 pandemic made this a painful lesson for some. It showed what it takes for a nonprofit to survive, and it exposed the organizations that could not operate sustainably or demonstrate relevancy.

During this time, many of our clients immediately went into scenario-planning mode. Some went into survival mode and had to determine potential losses and which expenses to cut. Even more went into hyperdrive, as the demand for their services rose significantly when people lost their jobs and had increased mental health or educational support needs. Their scenario planning looked different, as funders were seemingly throwing money at them to help meet the demand for their services.

Great leaders can adapt quickly and decisively to the unexpected. Doing thoughtful **scenario planning** during the budgeting process, however, will make the organization even more responsive and ready to adapt to the unexpected. The willingness to reevaluate practices and to change a mindset are critical survival skills for any nonprofit.

The Board of Directors' Role

I mentioned earlier that an organization's board of directors should approve its budget. Why is this important? The board of every nonprofit has legal duties, including accountability for the financial management and health of the organization. Board members and executive directors often do not understand the significance of this duty, but if you were to objectively view the structure as a business (a nonprofit *is* a corporation), ask yourself: *If the highest level of organizational leadership is not accountable for its financial well-being, who is?*

Board members must be fully informed and have **control mechanisms** in place to exercise their legal duties. As part of this role, the board should approve the budget, regularly review financial statements and uphold integrity in financial management.

Furthermore, nonprofit boards are accountable for the appropriation of funds, and funders have a right to hold a board accountable for mismanagement of grant funding. I have witnessed several nonprofits and their boards run into trouble because they misspent **restricted funds**, and the funders then exercised their right to request the funds be paid back. I have even seen a funder engage attorneys to pursue compliance of a grant contract. In this case, because the money was already spent, the shocked board now had to reraise those funds to pay the funder back.

When you sign a grant contract and accept funds, you are responsible for spending them according to the contract. As part of the grant application, some government agencies have started to require the board to submit a resolution saying that it understands its liability in ensuring that funds are spent as outlined in the grant contract.

We will talk more about board responsibilities in chapter 4, but it is important to impress that the board has a fiduciary responsibility that cannot be taken lightly.

Financial Reports Tell a Story about Your Organizational Health

It is vital that you utilize dynamic financial software to track and manage your organization's financial position. Like any other **data management system**, the information that can be extracted is only as good as the information that is entered. Financial management software enables an organization to segment out their revenue and expenses and track them against actuals. It also helps to analyze financial information and make informed revenue and expense projections, allowing for future planning and budgeting. Additionally, it has specific functions designed to help nonprofits, such as the ability to accept and track donations and keep track of donor receipts.

This system is different from your CRM (often referred to as a **donor database** or customer relationship management system); however, it is ideal and will save you a lot of time if the two systems sync up and share information. At the very least, they should be reconciled on a regular basis to ensure that no donation is falling through the cracks. If syncing is not possible, then donations should be entered into both systems, as they will be used by each system in a different way.

> **Financial management software enables an organization to segment out their revenue and expenses and track them against actuals.**

The financial software system will allow you to run important reports, including the **profit and loss statement** (sometimes called the P&L or Statement of Activities) and balance sheet (sometimes called a Statement of Financial Position). The P&L statement reflects actual expenses and revenue over a time period—typically year to date for the fiscal year. Funders compare this report to the organization's budget to determine whether it is on track toward the budgeted expenses and revenue.

If the P&L statement shows that the organization is not tracking appropriately toward budgeted projections, you need to be able to explain why. For example, if you know that a big donation is pending for the fourth quarter of your fiscal year, and that impacts the timing of cash flow, explain this to potential funders in your grant applications.

The balance sheet reports the assets, liabilities, and organization's equity at a specific point in time, giving a snapshot of a nonprofit's financial health. Funders use this to determine the amount of reserves (or cash on hand) an organization has. So if the organization's annual expense budget is $120,000, then you could divide that by twelve to determine a rough average monthly spend of $10,000 and then divide the cash balance on the balance sheet by this figure to determine the number of months of reserves the organization has. It is ideal for a typical organization to have a minimum of six months of cash reserves on hand but not more than eighteen months. If an organization has fewer than six months, it could look like a risky financial investment.

If the organization has more than eighteen months of cash reserves, the funder may think that it doesn't need the funding. We encourage you to look at how you can invest that back into your programs. Or if you are saving for a future *capital* need, move those funds into a capital funds account denoting the future purpose.

Every organization has to find its sweet spot in regard to a healthy cash reserve balance.

Otherwise, it will look like you are sitting on cash that could be invested in your programs, and funders are likely to pass you by in favor of a nonprofit that has a more immediate financial need. Every organization has to find its sweet spot in regard to a healthy cash reserve balance. Once you cross that threshold, it is time to look at long-term planning, **endowments**, and reinvestment in the organization.

Funders also look at the budget and financial reports to determine how diverse the revenue streams are. If more than 50 percent of your revenue is dependent on one source, and that source becomes unstable, your organization becomes unstable. Funders know this and are less likely to fund an organization without a strong mix of funding from different sources.

GETTING IT WISE: ADAPTING FINANCIAL SYSTEMS

For seven years, we worked with an organization whose founder envisioned making an impact on the lives of women and children who had survived domestic violence. Within the first five years, the organization went from serving up to twelve women and children at a time in a small single-family home to serving seventy women and children in a large multifamily campus. This phenomenal growth was a result of the dedication of active volunteers, charismatic visionary leadership, and fundraising.

When we first came on board, the agency was using QuickBooks. But it was using the program only to track expenses and accounts payable. There were no financial structures in place to track revenue or compare budgeted revenue and expenses to actuals. This limited its ability to apply for grants and subsequently track restricted revenue once funded.

We consulted with the agency's bookkeeper to explain how we needed reports to be run to submit them with grant applications, including adding the budget figures, segmenting their income and expenses appropriately, and establishing a financial reporting structure. When we helped the agency secure its first federal government grant—catalytic funding that doubled its revenue and tripled the number of families served—it had to further adapt its financial management systems to track restricted revenue and expenses through *subclasses*.

Your 990 Tells a Story about Financial Investment

Funders refer to your Form 990[2] to review your revenue, expenses, sources of revenue and how you spend your funds. While we are not *certified public accountants (CPAs)*, we have been interpreting nonprofit financials long enough to know when something doesn't look right. It is important that your CPA has a good understanding of nonprofit accounting and how to bucket expenses appropriately on Form 990, Section IX. Because your 990 is a public document, any interested donor can review your past 990s on GuideStar, a free online search tool that helps donors make informed investment decisions. This transparency promotes accountability, and you want to make

---

2   IRS Form 990 is a public document and must be filed by an organization exempt from income tax under section 501(a) if it has either (1) gross receipts greater than or equal to $200,000, or (2) total assets greater than or equal to $500,000 at the end of the tax year.

sure that this very public document tells an accurate story about your organization.

WISE REFERENCE

Charity Navigator, the world's largest and most-utilized independent nonprofit evaluator, believes that nonprofits spending less than one-third of their budget on program expenses are not living up to their mission and nonprofits spending less than 50 percent on program expenses receive a 0-star rating (on a 5-star scale) in terms of financial health. As a best practice, most nonprofits spend at least 75 percent of their budget on program expenses.[3]

Donors also use Charity Navigator and Charity Watch to review nonprofits. These sites rate and score organizations based on financial accountability and transparency. Spend time on them to ensure they have the right information about your organization and that you understand their rating criteria. Whether you consider these ratings fair or not, funders pay attention to them. If you have a high rating on Charity Navigator, make sure to promote that to current and prospective donors.

Some of our clients are ministries that are designated as church entities by the IRS, and therefore they are not required to file a 990. I always recommend that these organizations fill out 990s anyway (that they don't file with the IRS). These can be shared publicly on websites, on GuideStar, and with potential grant funders so that they have

---

3   Charity Navigator, "Financial Score Conversions and Tables," accessed August 24, 2021, https://www.charitynavigator.org/index.cfm?bay=content.view&cpid=48#Perf ormanceMetricOne.

the financial documents they are accustomed to reviewing. Donors appreciate this level of transparency.

A WISE CASE STUDY: CHILDREN'S ACADEMY

Children's Academy is a scrappy nonprofit that has been working to enrich the lives of children through childcare programming for more than twenty years. Its founder recognized this need in her low-income neighborhood at a young age, and since then, she has worked tirelessly to keep possibilities open for the children who live there. Like with many grassroots nonprofits, the academy's growth has been in direct response to the community's need—in this case, the need for safe, affordable and educational childcare.

The organization's primary funding comes from government tuition subsidies, which cover its essentials. When the executive director reached out to us in early 2019, the academy was facing a significant shift in how its programs were being funded, resulting in revenue instability. To make things worse, the arrival of the COVID-19 pandemic in early 2020 put its reliable stream of government subsidies in serious jeopardy, as the state continually recalculated funding and thousands of childcare agencies closed.

For the academy, diversifying its revenue had not historically been a high priority. And instead of bookkeeping, the academy was focused on the children's education. As a result, monthly bookkeeping tasks were typically months behind, financial reports were not reviewed on a regular basis, the budget was only very broadly outlined in a Microsoft Word document, and expense allocations were not tracked according to each program, making it difficult to adjust program spending based on changing needs. Our first step was to use the previous years' financial reports to help Children's Academy create a realistic organizational budget that the board could approve so that we could use it for grant applications.

Children's Academy also needed improved financial accounting. We connected the academy with a vetted accounting professional with nonprofit expertise and coordinated conversations to facilitate the update of its financial accounting software, including the creation of a chart of accounts that not only met its organizational needs but helped with more targeted **grant writing** strategies.

When we reviewed **IRS Form 990**, Section IX, for Children's Academy, we realized that its CPA must not be experienced in nonprofit accounting. What tipped us off? Its 990 reflected that more than 50 percent of its budget was spent on administrative expenses. As we became familiar with the academy's programming, we knew there was no way it was spending 50 percent of its expenses on administrative costs. This mistake on a 990 can have a significant impact on funding opportunities, as funders often look at administrative, programs, and fundraising expense ratios to determine whether they will invest. An unknowing CPA may not understand the importance of making sure that these ratios are correct.

The executive director of the Children's Academy was open to coaching and adapting their financial systems at every turn. A combination of the academy's adaptability, relevance, resilience, and improved financial tracking netted the agency $223,021 (23 percent of its revenue) in new funding in 2020. It is still opening doors and possibilities for the community, while many other nonprofits have been forced to close.

Your 990 provides other important information to the public. It lists the salaries of your top-paid staff and any compensation you provide to board members. It should be noted that it is not common to compensate board members of public charities. Funders may review staff salaries and whether the board is compensated to make a judgment call about how you spend donor dollars.

WISE PRO TIP: JOB SEEKERS REVIEW YOUR 990

Smart job seekers will refer to your 990 to see what you pay your executive leaders to determine an appropriate salary offer or whether they will even apply for a position.

An Audit Tells the Story of Financial Integrity

If you have intentions of seeking major grant funding, we strongly encourage you to perform an annual *financial audit*, especially if you have a budget over $250,000. An audit is conducted by a CPA and provides an analysis and verification of the financial affairs of an organization over a given time frame, typically the organization's fiscal year.

Audits are often required by major funders such as United Way, government agencies, and even some corporate and private foundations. Some institutional funders will not consider a grant request without an audit attached. Getting one can pay dividends, while not having an audit can mean leaving money on the table. It is a board decision that is dependent on the organization's growth and funding goals.

Some organizations seeking limited grant funding that does not require an audit opt to get a *financial statement review* instead of an audit. In a review, an accountant obtains *limited assurance* that there are no *material modifications* that need to be made to an entity's financial statements for them to be in conformity with *GAAP* accounting standards. A review does not require the accountant to obtain an understanding of *internal controls* or to assess fraud risk or other types of audit

> Financial reviews and audits give credibility to an organization's financial statements and provide the stakeholders confidence that the accounts are true and fair–telling the story that you care about your organization's financial integrity.

level assurances. A review is more expensive than a *financial compilation report* (financial statements compiled without any assurance on the statements) and less expensive than an audit.

Financial reviews and audits give credibility to an organization's financial statements and provide the stakeholders (e.g., board members and donors) confidence that the accounts are true and fair—telling the story that you care about your organization's financial integrity.

A WISE CAUTIONARY TALE: TO AUDIT OR NOT TO AUDIT

Early in my consulting career, I sat in on a board meeting of one of my clients. The board chair was the founder, and the board members were his friends. I had repeatedly recommended to the chair that they commission an audit, and those conversations led to a board discussion. One of the board members turned to the board chair and said, "Audits are only necessary if we don't trust you, and we do trust you. So it isn't worth the $15,000 expense." The rest of the board agreed.

I was stunned. Yes, audits confirm the organization's books are true and fair, but that doesn't mean they are based on distrust. If the books are off, that doesn't mean they've been cooked. It means that errors have been made and you can now recognize them and find your way back to balance.

This perspective on the board's part is risky and shortsighted, as it is the board's duty to ensure the financial health of the organization. Trust and respect won't save the organization or defend the board in a **breach of duty** situation, when **financial malfeasance** occurs. When this does happen, most victims are blindsided by it. No one expects someone they trust to steal.

An important note: If your audit has findings and you receive a **management letter** outlining those findings, it is important that you have a response letter signed by your board chair to include with the audit and the management letter when submitting it to funders. This response letter outlines how your organization will correct the audit findings moving forward. Then, make sure you *implement* the changes outlined in your response letter. Funders may excuse a management letter once, but they likely will not excuse repeated letters outlining audit findings that are never addressed.

WISE PRO TIP: EXPLAIN A DEFICIT

We recommend that if your audit reflects a deficit or other concerning financial situation, you craft a statement to include in the audit report to explain it. This statement about the cause of a deficit is critical to have on hand when submitting grant applications, as this is a question you will have to answer frequently.

Word to the WISE

Now you know that your financials tell a story. As a board-approved, static document, your budget tells a story about planning and foresight. Your financial reports provide insight into the financial health of your organization, and your 990 provides insight into how you invest your resources. The audit tells a story about financial integrity. Altogether these financial documents are reviewed by funders to determine whether your organization is a worthy investment. Take some time to review your financial documents and systems to determine whether there are areas for improvement that will help you tell a more accurate and compelling story.

CHAPTER

3

PITFALL ③

Your Funding Is Not Sustainable

As you know from chapter 1, sustainability is the key to your stool's fundraising leg being structurally sound. In this chapter, we will explore how to avoid the pitfall of focusing on revenue strategies that are not sustainable: lack of diversification of revenue, limited individual giving, and the lack of a *return on investment (ROI)* on fundraising strategies.

A WISE CASE STUDY: A PERFECT STORM

Front Line Mental Health Services became the perfect storm.

This nonprofit had been providing mental health services for thirty years. But somewhere along the way, its leadership had started to spend its reserves and endowment, rely too heavily on restricted grant funds, and make too many urgent crisis appeals, creating **donor fatigue**.

Front Line hired me in mid-June to help execute two major fundraising events—a golf tournament in September and a luncheon in March—during a time when its development department was experiencing staff turnover. As I assessed the events, I noticed they had historically high expense ratios, so I aimed to bring expenses in line with industry standards of 25 percent or less. The tournament, a new event, had no committed sponsors or teams, just a loosely assembled **event committee** of men who liked to play golf. The luncheon was in the early stages of planning.

At first, we looked at ways we could encourage sponsors to give to both events in a combination sponsorship appeal. But the luncheon had usually been sponsored by individuals, and golf tournaments typically rely on corporate support. So we dropped this idea.

When implementing a new event, especially within a short time frame, look to leverage your existing relationships as much as possible. This is when a committee is vital—so you can tap into members' networks. Unfortunately, Front Line's golf committee was not enthusiastic about fundraising, and as the event drew closer, there was no way we could meet the contracted minimum number of player registrations. The event was going to lose money.

Meanwhile, one of Front Line's other events, this one for young professionals, was projected to barely break even. This was usually a well-attended event, and while it didn't bring in funds, it was raising awareness, and according to the executive director, that was important too.

Fewer than two months into my work with Front Line, the executive director left, and the vice president of programs stepped in to serve as the interim executive director. Around this time, I attended a board meeting to discuss the upcoming events and what support was needed from board members. There, as the new treasurer went over the organization's financial position, I carefully reviewed its financial statements. The cash balance was extremely low, and it appeared the board had nearly decimated the last of its reserves to pay half of a $90,000 speaker fee for the luncheon. I was surprised no one was talking about any of this with any sense of urgency.

After the meeting, I asked the new interim executive director about Front Line's cash position. When she reached out to me later, she was in a panic. The organization didn't have enough money to make it through the next two months. Not only that, but they also had been shuffling restricted gifts around to cover operational expenses, like administrative salaries. They needed cash fast!

There were many factors that led to Front Line's situation. At its core was an overreliance on restricted revenue: 59 percent of its budget was funded by restricted grants. Meanwhile, the amount of unrestricted revenue coming in wasn't able to cover operational infrastructure at the rate the organization was spending money.

In this situation, those members of the board with financial expertise who had tried to call attention to the financial crisis were pushed out or resigned, and many others blindly trusted an executive director who presented incomplete financial information in the most favorable way possible. (We talked about how dangerous this is in the last chapter. It is imperative that board members know how to interpret financial documents and ask hard questions, so they can make informed decisions.)

When we realized how serious Front Line's financial situation was, we brought together several well-connected board members, a crisis communications consultant, and another nonprofit strategy consultant. Our game plan involved targeted one-on-one conversations with Front Line's most dedicated donors. Hope turned to heartbreak, however, when one frustrated donor after the other said being asked for crisis support was an all-too-frequent occurrence.

Why was the organization in a seemingly constant state of funding crisis? Repeatedly, we heard, "I love the organization, but I no longer trust that my donation will be enough to turn this around." Donor fatigue had set in. (Organizations should only use crisis appeals sparingly. Otherwise, donors no longer believe that your crisis is real. *Don't forget: People want to be part of a winning team. No one wants to jump aboard a sinking ship.*)

As the days ticked by, it became more apparent that Front Line may no longer be financially viable. It began to reach out to merger prospects to preserve its programs, plan for a possible shutdown, talk to funders of restricted grants about releasing the restrictions, and mull a layoff of more than twenty employees.

This experience was devastating for everyone involved. The organization filled a service that was in high demand. But its fundraising leg was crippled. In the end, it was forced to not only close its doors but also pay back funds from one of its restricted grants. All this happened within ninety days of the interim executive director discovering Front Line's financial mess.

Organizational sustainability requires diverse revenue streams, strong cash reserves, and a long-term funding strategy that focuses on building unrestricted revenue. It also requires being good stewards of resources. When an organization experiences financial challenges, it must revert to spending conservatively—ensuring every dollar can be linked to impact or building resources. Front Line's $90,000 speaker fee was not a justifiable expense, especially when it meant spending the last of the organization's financial resources—nor was knowingly implementing events that operated at a loss.

Make Grant Funding Work Best for You

In our case study, Front Line was primarily funded by grants, leading to a common pitfall of being overly reliant on them. Let's dive into how to make them work best for you.

One of WISE's largest service lines is grant writing. Grants are a funding source people often associate with nonprofits, and they are often a revenue stream on which nonprofits rely too heavily, making them vulnerable to the changing interests of a small number of funders.

Still, grants can be the catalytic power behind organizational growth. I encourage nonprofits to utilize grants as expansion or capacity-building funds. Grant funding can also be an invaluable part of an annual fundraising plan when part of a diversified mix of revenue.

> **Growing nonprofits can make the mistake of building their identities around available grant funding.**

Sometimes growing nonprofits can make the mistake of building their identities around available grant funding. I have seen organizations design an entirely new program that doesn't align with their mission or current programming just to capture funds. This *money chasing* causes them to exhaust operational resources in order to implement a program that may not even be sustainable. Money chasing also indicates **mission creep** and often results in programming reliant on a single funding source with no backup plan for when that funding is discontinued.

Another mistake nonprofits make is overly restricting their funding with an ask that's too narrow. A childcare center that requests a grant for $20,000 to purchase a climbing wall could be losing out on money by making such a specific request. If the funder likes to fund "stuff," or capital needs, this could be the right ask. But if the funder likes to fund programs, the organization has just restricted those funds unnecessarily; it could have widened the ask to fund its childcare or health and wellness outdoor programs. That way, the funds could be used to cover any expenses within that broader program budget.

There are ways to ask for the least restrictive funding possible. If you have a chance to ask for **general operating expenses**, go for it. Ask to use the funding on the organization's greatest need and that the funder trust your qualified ability to determine its best use. Fortunately, more funders are recognizing that funding for salaries is vital to supporting the organization's mission. After all, talent is the most valuable asset for achieving it.

That brings us to the "How much?" question, which also brings us back to budgeting. If you want to know how much money to ask for a program, you need to know how much that program really costs. The program budget you submit should be as comprehensive as possible. Unlike organizational budgets, program budgets are more flexible (they don't need to be board-approved static documents— you are only committed to the program budget projections if you receive funding for it), and for grant-writing purposes, they should be developed with best-case scenarios in mind. In addition to staff and equipment, include every potential expense, such as postage, supplies, computer and internet, marketing, mileage, professional development and training, program evaluation, and data collection and management.

Because your program probably also depends on administrative support, include a portion of your operating expenses (also referred to as administrative expenses), such as insurance, building and grounds maintenance, and administrative personnel (HR, accounting, etc.). If a program budget is 30 percent of your organization's overall budget, then 30 percent of its operating expenses can be included in the program budget. For example, if the program budget is $100,000 and the organization's overall budget is $300,000, the program budget makes up 33 percent of the overall budget. Now if administrative expenses are $60,000, then 33 percent of $60,000 is $19,800 and this would give you a program budget of $119,800. The administrative costs make up about 16.5 percent of the program budget. Some funders, especially government funders, may restrict the amount of administrative expenses you can include in a program budget to 5 or 10 percent. Always include administrative expenses in program budgets unless a funder specifically says not to.

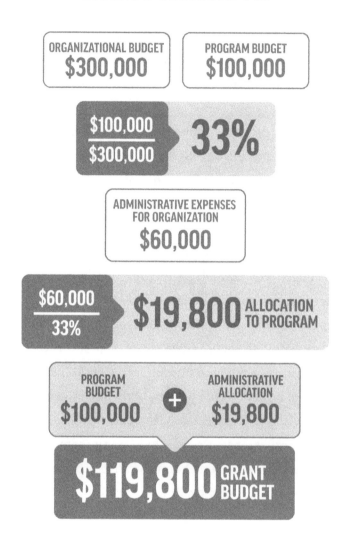

As mentioned in chapter 1, you should also add in expenses provided in-kind to your program budget, especially if you hope to have them funded in the future. Say a nonprofit has a program budget of $100,000, but that doesn't include the executive director's salary because they are volunteering their time. Here, you would determine the position's salary as if you were paying it and include the appropriate percentage of the salary in your program ask. If the executive director's salary should be $75,000 (market rate), and they spend 25 percent of their time on the program, then $18,750 should be included in the program budget.[4]

The goal is to provide a funder with an understanding of the full cost of your program and give you the opportunity to request the maximum amount possible within the grant's guidelines. Remember that when you receive a grant, you are committing to spend it on the budget that you presented with the grant application unless you make different arrangements with the funder.

> **When you receive a grant, you are committing to spend it on the budget that you presented with the grant application unless you make different arrangements with the funder.**

WISE PRO TIP: RIGHTSIZE YOUR PROGRAM BUDGET

Make sure that your program budget is rightsized with your organizational budget. If you have a program budget that is $1 million and your organizational budget or historical revenue/expenses are closer to $200,000, you'll need to be able explain to a funder how (and why) you plan to make that large of a leap in implementing or growing a program budget.

EXPLORING GOVERNMENT GRANTS

As noted, nonprofits can get themselves into a jam by chasing funds and becoming overly reliant on a single funding source. This can occur when government grants are involved as well. Often, government

---

4   Keep in mind that program budgets you submit to funders have this level of flexibility, and GAAP accounting standards have different requirements for 990 reporting and audit purposes. (Consult your CPA for details.)

agencies are most interested in outcomes and outputs and not whether your entire budget has become dependent on government funding.

Different sources of government funding exist, including city, county, state, and federal. It is important to understand where the funds come from and the goals of that agency. Frequently, local government grant opportunities are federal funds funneled through a local agency acting as a grant administrator.

When considering a government grant opportunity, attend associated webinars, and follow all application guidelines meticulously. Check online for any question-and-answer postings, and take advantage of any Q&A sessions.

When you are weighing whether a government grant opportunity is right for your organization, consider the following.

Is It Worth It?

When it comes to grants of $50,000 or less, we often discourage a client from applying if they cannot easily comply with all the requirements associated with the grant. This is because sometimes the effort that goes into meeting the reporting and programmatic requirements offsets the value of the award.

WISE PRO TIP: MAKE SURE THE GRANT SIZE MAKES SENSE

In our process, we try to ascertain the ease with which our client can implement the grant within its current operating and program structure and whether it has the necessary financial systems in place for reporting. If the nonprofit must implement a new program with the grant funds, then it must have the total funding needed to implement the program. Let's say the grant award is $50,000, and because the nonprofit will need to implement a new program, there must be another committed source of funds to take care of the rest of the program cost. (Additionally, $50,000 is unlikely to be enough to launch a new program.) But if the nonprofit is large and this opportunity fits well into its current programming, there are fewer hurdles, and we would be more likely to encourage it to apply.

Can You Afford It?

Most government grants reimburse expenses. This means you must spend the money first, keep detailed records of the expenses, and then submit a request for reimbursement. Sometimes it takes months to receive it. Nonprofits without appropriate levels of cash on hand can be highly burdened by this delay.

Also important to note is that many government grants, particularly those involving federal funds, require a match. This match is usually 20 percent, and the receiving organization must bring these funds to the table as part of the grant award. If your grant award is $100,000 and includes a 20 percent match, you are on the hook for $20,000.

Additionally, if you receive a federal grant of $750,000 or more, you are required to perform a *single audit*, which could cost your organization $10,000 or more. This expense is not usually covered by the grant.

Do You Have the Tools and Capacity to Track Metrics and Financials?

Some federal grant applications now require you to sign an **attestation** that you have the ability to track restricted grants and budgeted expenses versus actuals. Managing government grants means that your financial systems need to be highly sophisticated, which may require you to overhaul your systems and hire an experienced nonprofit bookkeeper. The attestation may also hold you to tracking metrics and outcomes.

Finally, if the grant covers any portion of salaries, you are required to track 100 percent of that salaried person's time, and those time sheets must reflect the corresponding percentage of time spent on the grant-funded program (anything less means a loss of funding). If you have asked for 100 percent of an employee's salary to be funded by the grant, *all* their activities must be associated with that grant-funded program.

Can You Commit to the Requirements?

When we review a grant opportunity for a client, we spend two to three hours reading the **request for proposals (RFPs)**, including every attachment. This helps us create a **project plan** that outlines all activities and requirements associated with the grant and assigns deadlines and the person responsible. We share and review this plan with the client, along with any programmatic or organizational requirements they need to follow to receive the funding. This time investment is important, as government applications are complicated and requirements can be buried in attachments. Funders don't pay when a regulated program is out of compliance, so you need to be confident that you can follow their requirements and that you have tracking and **quality controls** in place.

OVERRELIANCE ON GOVERNMENT GRANTS IS RISKY

Nonprofits with budgets that are highly funded by government grants or programs—sometimes as high as 90 percent—are left trying to fill the funding difference, which is usually administrative expenses. Raising funds for administrative expenses and for a program that is already 90 percent funded is a challenge because foundations (and individual donors) rarely want to fund administrative expenses, and when they are reviewing your nonprofit against your competitors who have less "guaranteed" revenue, guess who they are going to fund?

Putting so many of your eggs in one basket in this way has another effect: it can cultivate fundraising complacency. This is a mindset in which you're satisfied with raising just enough funding to fill the gap—not focused on diversifying revenue and cultivating relationships with individual donors. This kind of complacency can impact the organization's long-term sustainability.

What happens when that government funding goes away? Let's say you lose that contract, and the organization must shutter a program—but all stakeholders are OK with that. In this case, backup funding isn't needed. But if that program is important to the organization, to the ongoing implementation of the mission, and for what you're trying to accomplish in the community, then you will definitely need backup funding sources. The best way to obtain them is to have a strong strategy when it comes to diversifying revenue streams with unrestricted revenue. Use the stability of government funding to give you an opportunity to proactively diversify revenue, primarily through individual-giving strategies. This sustainability strategy is often overlooked to the point of no return. You can't lose your government funding one day and expect to immediately springboard into an individual-giving campaign the next.

Funding Diversity: The 33 Percent Guide

Just as I have stressed the dangers of overreliance on grants, the same holds true for depending too heavily on any single (or two) stream(s) of income. This scenario often exists when nonprofits first get off the ground through large donations from one or two *angel donors*. Like angel investors in the for-profit world, these are donors who buy into the vision of the organization's founder and demand very little proof of initial impact. Having this early support is beneficial but is not sustainable. A nonprofit should have a plan to wean itself from angel donors within three years or fewer.

> **Each organization's funding breakdown will be different, but the 33 percent rule is a good guide to follow.**

Diverse funding streams are key to financial sustainability. Any nonprofit relying on one source (one grant, one donor, one event) for more than 50 percent of its total funding is financially at risk. Ideally, funding streams would break down to at least 33 percent in individual giving and a maximum of 33 percent each in grants and events/corporate giving. Each organization's funding breakdown will be different, but the 33 percent rule is a good guide to follow.

When it comes to your individual donor base, the larger, the better. If you have two thousand donors who, on average, donate $100 a year, that's $200,000. It's an established base to continually build upon. Even though donor attrition will occur, you can limit this through thoughtful donor *stewardship*. The key is to have hundreds or thousands of dedicated individual donors as opposed to just a handful of donors giving large gifts.

GETTING IT WISE: WEANING OFF ANGEL DONORS

A Place Called Home knew how to grow its donor base. This small nonprofit launched with two angel donors who believed in the mission to serve single mothers struggling with housing insecurity. From the outset, it had a strategy to wean itself from its angel donors in three to five years. And that's exactly what A Place Called Home did. How? By getting its board and executive team to introduce their friends to the organization and then asking current donors to introduce them to others who might be interested in the mission.

Board members held small meet-and-greet events and invited their friends for a happy hour and a tour of the program and then asked them to give to the organization. Sometimes, they would ask their friends to make a donation to A Place Called Home in lieu of a birthday or holiday gift. Hearing a friend say, "I believe in/donate to/volunteer for this organization, and here's why"—that's powerful.

When leaders from A Place Called Home asked us to work with them on a capital campaign, we were amazed to find that 90 percent of its funding came from individuals. They had yet to apply for grants. This was an optimal situation. They had untapped resources in grant funders, and they could demonstrate to those funders the wide net they'd cast when it came to individual giving. If A Place Called Home had instead been overly reliant on grant funding, it would've had to return to those same funders, potentially cannibalizing the funding it's dependent on to fund programming or operational expenses.

Maximizing Special Events

Front Line's case study highlights the dangers of squandering resources on events. I started my career as a special event fundraiser for organizations like the Cystic Fibrosis Foundation and American Heart Association. I firmly believe that events serve a valuable role in fundraising. And if implemented strategically, they can be a terrific source of unrestricted revenue and an entry point for new donors. Here's how to maximize special events for your organization.

YOUR PRIMARY GOAL IS TO RAISE FUNDS

The purpose of a fundraising event is to bring in money for your mission. Raising awareness is a secondary benefit. When determining the return on investment of a popular event, and you are breaking even on revenue versus expenses—take the young professionals' event put on by Front Line, for example—you are actually losing money once you consider the value of staff and volunteer time. When you start justifying the event by saying its primary purpose is to raise awareness, it's time to sunset that event.

MAXIMIZE ROI

According to industry best practices, the maximum amount that should be spent on event expenses is 25 percent of gross revenue. This doesn't include staff time, which is important to consider when determining the long-term viability of any fundraising strategy. If your fundraising staff or volunteers are spending their time primarily focused on activities that are not generating revenue, moneymaking opportunities are falling through the cracks. Every aspect of an event should contribute to its overall ROI, including games and entertainment. Perform a cost/benefit analysis. For example, silent auctions are fun,

> According to industry best practices, the maximum amount that should be spent on event expenses is 25 percent of gross revenue.

but if a donated $90 Instapot is handled eleven times by volunteers before it sells for $30, is this the best use of resources?

HOLD THE BOARD ACCOUNTABLE

"ABC Nonprofit made six figures with their golf tournament. We should do one!" suggests the board. Yet not even one member secures a sponsor or recruits teams. Sound familiar? Setting expectations for board involvement and providing step-by-step guides and **collateral materials** will help members be successful in supporting events. Consider having at least one board member on the event planning committee who will hold the other board members accountable for their support.

MAJOR FUNDRAISING EVENTS TAKE A FULL YEAR TO IMPLEMENT

Do you want to know how those other nonprofits are raising $1 million or more on their event? They work on it all year long. The greatest mistake you can make with an event is waiting to start working on it. This was a contributing factor of the downfall of Front Line. In some cases, they waited three to six months before an event to start working on it. By that point, they were in crisis mode.

WISE PRO TIP: NEVER STOP CULTIVATING EVENT SPONSORS

Cultivating event sponsors is also a year-round activity. The best time to begin securing sponsorships for next year's event is immediately after this year's event! If you recommit all your sponsors within three months of your successful event, then you have at least six months to focus on securing new ones. All sponsors—corporations and individuals—have annual budgets. Your goal is to be the first sponsorship they are excited to put in their budget. If you wait until January to ask for sponsorship for an April event, you've likely missed the fall budgeting season altogether. The ultimate win: Reach your sponsorship goal (better yet, sell out with sponsorship) three months out from your event, and then spend those three months focused on making sure it will be the best event experience possible.

UTILIZE AN EVENT COMMITTEE

We often hear that event committees are too much work to manage, and it's just easier for staff to do everything. If managed effectively, volunteer committees can be the key to your event's success. Consider this: You are one person, with your own sphere of connections and time availability. But with a committee of dedicated volunteers, you multiply your network and your capacity! Crucial here is being clear about expectations from the very beginning (during recruitment) so that they understand they're committing to achieving a fundraising goal. (We will dig more into how to build your fundraising dream team in chapter 5.)

HAVE A PLAN FOR ONGOING CULTIVATION

Special events are entry points for new donors. Have a cultivation strategy you trigger immediately following an event to engage guests— invite them on a tour or to volunteer. Don't let them wait to hear from you again the next time the event rolls around (or even worse, never).

As with other types of funding, don't rely on one single event or allow most of your budget to be dependent on event revenue. During the pandemic, clients who had more than 50 percent of their revenue come from events suffered quite a bit, even when they pivoted to virtual events. Many lost massive amounts of funding from sponsorship and event fee revenue. If you are in this situation, make a plan to diversify your revenue with a focus on individual giving. If you are holding on to a fundraising strategy that does not have a positive ROI, it's time to either get more serious about return or shut it down.

A WISE CAUTIONARY TALE: IF YOU BUILD IT … THEY MAY *NOT* COME

Successful fundraising efforts require you to live your brand and position yourself and your organization as *thought leaders* in your mission space.

At Volunteers of America Texas (VOATX), I raised funds to support life-changing work with the Working Families Success Network (WFSN) model[5] at our site in Houston. There, we were

---

5   Developed by the Annie E. Casey Foundation, the WFSN model helps low-income individuals and families get on a path to financial stability. At the center of this is the coordination of key services at convenient locations, which makes these resources more accessible to those needing assistance. In 2013, funders and organizations throughout the country formed the Working Families Sucess Network.

making great strides with the model, helping individuals newly released from prison find sustainable living wage employment.

As a statewide agency, VOATX wanted to expand this highly successful model by bringing it to Dallas. To do so, we looked to the United Way of Metropolitan Dallas, which offered funding opportunities for workforce development, financial education, and basic needs. All three of these funding streams directly correlated with the WFSN model. At the time, United Way's application process required nonprofits to apply for each of these funding areas separately, as the integrated services model wasn't common in Dallas. So I wrote three different applications—each one focusing on the specific program funding area while explaining that the model we used was a validated one-stop-shop program supported nationally by the Annie E. Casey Foundation. This was an evidence-based, life-changing program with the outcomes to prove it, and we were doing it successfully. I was excited—I mean, we were a shoo-in, right?

We didn't get the money. United Way declined our application because even though VOATX is a one-hundred-plus-year-old organization, we hadn't established ourselves or built a reputation with funders in the Dallas area yet. We didn't have credibility, especially not enough to assert the merits of a program model that wasn't well known by local funders. While the United Way staff were familiar with it, the volunteers vetting the applications had never heard of it (or us) before. They were confused about how it worked and what the one-stop-shop program was.

I often share this story with nonprofits poised to make the same mistake I did—that believing good work and demonstrated impact should easily result in money for your programs. The lesson here, however: You must establish credibility. You could have the most impactful programs in the community, but you must position yourself as a thought leader and expert in your mission space. That means if there are meetings in the community related to your mission, be there.

It took two years, but VOATX finally established itself enough in the Dallas market. We received funding from a major funder who was investing in North Texas nonprofits to incubate the WFSN model. Leading up to that big win, I was everywhere our potential stakeholders were. I kept showing up, connecting and building our credibility until they trusted us enough to fund us.

Word to the WISE

Learn from Front Line's mistakes, and avoid the pitfall of relying on unsustainable fundraising strategies. You may already know where you need to make some tough decisions right away. Spend some time reviewing your funding mix and the return on investment for your fundraising strategies. As we move through the next chapters, you'll learn more about how to appeal to individual donors and diversify your revenue.

CHAPTER 4

PITFALL **4**

Your Board Is Asleep at the Wheel

Front Line Mental Health Services is a case study of an established agency that lost its viability as a nonprofit corporation. As I shared in chapter 3, Front Line closed after thirty years in large part because its board was not paying attention to agency financials. Sometimes this happens when board members don't know how to interpret financials or are overly reliant on the executive director to make decisions regarding spending. This is rubber-stamping at its most dangerous.

The Disengaged Board

Nonprofit governance has a dual focus: achieving the organization's social mission and ensuring the organization is viable. Both responsibilities relate to fiduciary responsibility that a board of trustees has with respect to the exercise of authority over the explicit actions the organization takes. Public trust and accountability is an essential aspect of organizational viability, so it achieves the social mission in a way that is respected by those whom the organization serves and the society in which it is located.[6]

—NONPROFIT QUARTERLY

The most common complaints we hear executive directors make about their boards are that members are not engaged, they're not helping raise money, and they don't understand how things work in the organization. At this point, I ask:

- Do they have a **job description** (in addition to the bylaws)?
- What does the onboarding process look like?
- What kind of training have they received?

It's not enough to simply believe your nonprofit's mission is important; you must demonstrate that belief by setting high standards for your board and providing members with the necessary tools to meet those standards.

A lack of board engagement almost always stems from the recruiting and onboarding process, or lack thereof. If your recruitment strategy is to get your friends to become board members by telling them they don't need to do much, then that's exactly what you'll get—people who don't do much.

Also, for your part, it's not enough to simply believe your non-

---

6   "What Is Governance? A Guide for Nonprofits on Board Governance," nonprofit-quarterly.org (*Nonprofit Quarterly*, July 17, 2018), https://nonprofitquarterly.org/what-is-governance-definition/#:~:text=Nonprofit%20governance%20has%20a%20dual,ensuring%20the%20organization%20is%20viable.

profit's mission is important; you must demonstrate that belief by setting high standards for your board and providing members with the necessary tools to meet those standards. A clear structure, high expectations, and ongoing accountability create an environment where people feel valued and understand their importance to the organization and its mission.

A BOARD OF DIRECTORS HAS LEGAL DUTIES

A WISE CAUTIONARY TALE: BOARD MEMBERS CAN BE HELD PERSONALLY LIABLE FOR A NONPROFIT'S CONDUCT

I know someone who won a multimillion-dollar lawsuit against individual board members of a nonprofit organization. The claim accused the nonprofit's CEO of fraudulent behavior when he withheld a child's health information during an adoption the organization was facilitating. During the case, an investigation revealed that the board was made aware of this activity through a series of emails. Each board member who was copied on these emails was named independently in the suit. In the end, they were held personally liable for the organization's fraudulent behavior and were required to pay for it—with big dollars. (It also should be noted here that directors' and officers' insurance does not cover willful fraud.)

The board exists to act as the informed voice and agent of the owners in both a legal and moral sense. While for-profit boards receive their authority from shareholders, nonprofit ones receive their authority from public stakeholders of the mission. As such, board members cannot delegate their legal duties of care, obedience, and loyalty. If a member does not exercise responsibilities with due diligence, they could be held legally liable for the actions of an organization.

Say you are a board member named in a lawsuit. Your legal liability would be evaluated using the business judgment rule: If you do your best to make a decision in a thoughtful way and it goes wrong, you can be excused from liability. But if it was done without due diligence, you can be held accountable.

A WISE CAUTIONARY TALE: LEAVE FRIENDSHIPS AT THE DOOR

One of the most common causes of a disengaged board is when it is made up of friends of the founder or executive director. Often in this environment, board members don't perform their fiduciary duties and don't hold the executive director or each other accountable. How can they when friendship is the priority?

Previously, I worked for an organization in which the executive director had recruited 90 percent of the board. The organization was a local, independent 501(c)(3) under an *affiliate* agreement with a national nonprofit. When more than ten staff members became whistleblowers about the executive director to the national office, it allowed the local board to investigate the allegations and take corrective action. This local board (friends of the executive director) allowed the executive director to vet and hire the third-party firm chosen to conduct the investigation.

What's more, when the HR director conducted an exit interview with a staff member who revealed information about the executive director, he turned the interview transcript over to the board chair (the direct supervisor of the executive director), who chastised the

HR director for not being loyal to the executive director and then promptly shared the interview *with* the executive director.

Ultimately, the national office revoked the **charter** of the affiliate and removed the executive director and the local board. While this may seem like an extreme example, it is not uncommon for friendships between board members and the CEO or founder to eclipse responsibilities.

The Engaged Board

The board of directors is the highest level of leadership in the organization. It is their job to:

- protect the mission and ensure activities are in alignment

- conduct strategic planning

- hire, manage, and evaluate the chief executive officer (CEO or executive director)

- ensure leadership succession plans are in place

- ensure the organization has the necessary resources to operate

- provide fiduciary oversight and financial management

- support and monitor program performance and service delivery

- assess and improve board performance

- ensure organizational credibility, ethics, and brand protection and

- reduce organizational risk

Individual board members must exercise care, loyalty, and obedience. This includes:

- Being active in attendance and engagement

- Preparing for board meetings

- Speaking up on legal, ethical or financial concerns

- Serving on committees

- Being knowledgeable about the organization's mission, programs, services, policies, and clients

- Addressing any conflicts of interest

- Being informed ambassadors for the organization

- Making personal and meaningful financial contributions

- Identifying and cultivating new board members

- Utilizing skills for the betterment of the organization

EFFECTIVE BYLAWS

Bylaws guide how the board governs the organization and include the following:

- General organization information, such as the mission and location of services

- A statement of purpose (mission)

- A list of leadership positions and how they are elected

- Number of board members

- Meeting and voting procedures

- Service term and term limits

- Conflict-of-interest policy

- *Give-get policy*

- Committee charters

- Dissolution process and provisions for amending bylaws (bylaws should be reviewed annually and updated when needed)

INTENTIONAL RECRUITMENT

For the sake of the mission, the board must be committed and well equipped to exercise its legal duties with a representation of diverse perspectives, lived experience, and the skills and talents needed to steer the strategic direction of the nonprofit. This is best accomplished with a formal recruitment process, board training, and accountability mechanisms.

First, determine the skills and experience you need on the board. A successful one requires the right combination of leadership qualities, areas of expertise, community connections, and diverse perspectives. Use a **board matrix** to design your ideal board. It is a tool used to outline a nonprofit's needs for board representation and serves as your road map to building and maintaining your cabinet of strategic advisors. Common areas of focus on a board matrix include the following:

- Areas of expertise, such as administration, legal, human resources, and strategic planning

- Resources, such as the personal financial means to donate, access to resources, and experience with fundraising

- *Social capital*, such as access to other services, media, and religious institutions

- Personal style of service, such as consensus builder, visionary, strategist, and tactical worker

- *Demographics*, including age, gender, race/ethnicity, geography, and experience

The demographics of your board should be representative of the individuals you serve and include lived experience with your mission. Using a matrix to establish an intentional recruitment strategy fosters board diversity. If your board recruitment strategy involves relying on board members to recruit their friends, your board will likely be a homogeneous group of people without diverse representation or thought. People tend to socialize with people like themselves.

In addition to filling a gap in the matrix, prospective board members should

- be passionate about the mission and organization

- be willing to make a serious commitment of time, treasure, and talent

- be knowledgeable about the organization's mission and services

- be credible and demonstrate sound judgment

- be willing and capable of bringing resources to the organization, and

- have the ability to influence others

This process of assessing and developing your board is not just for new nonprofits. It is an ongoing need for nonprofits in all stages of the *organizational life cycle*.

Now you know who you are looking for and can begin to recruit meaningfully. Utilize circles of influence—who do you know? Who do they know? Other sources of board members include:

- Current volunteers (look at committees, advisory boards, highly engaged program volunteers)

- Current and prospective funders

- Influential community or corporate leadership

- Community groups that build volunteer leaders like Junior League

- Social media networks

- Client connections

- Social or civic clubs

- Chambers of commerce

- Churches

- Trade associations

- Universities

The recruitment process should be formal. The governance committee often serves as the nominating committee. While all board members are encouraged to recommend potential board candidates, it is the governance committee that makes the first formal contact, providing the prospect with a clear picture of the role and determining the level of interest. The committee reports back to the board, and if the board approves, the prospect is invited to formally apply. Yes, potential board members must apply for this valued position!

A formal application signifies the importance of the role. It should come with a comprehensive overview of responsibilities, along with required competencies and commitments. It should also request a signature of understanding and agreement to the terms of the role. Never downplay expectations or soft-pitch a board commitment. Demanding the best from your board members reflects your commitment to the mission and the organization's long-term success and sustainability.

Once an application is received, there should be a formal interview or screening process. Have each interviewer use a standardized candidate assessment form to record input. This step is important. Just like in hiring a staff position, you have one shot to get the right board members "hired" for the job. If there is not a vacancy, a qualified applicant should be encouraged to become a member of one of the board committees. These groups do not have to be made up of just board members and are a great way to initiate individuals into the organization and to assess their commitment and engagement level before offering a board role.

FORMAL ONBOARDING

Once the governance committee has completed the screening process, there should be an official vote of the board to bring on the new member, and then the onboarding process begins. This process is critical to the success of new board members.

Each member should be provided a board handbook that includes the following at a minimum:

- Articles of incorporation

- Bylaws

- Job description

- Contact list of all board members

- Organizational chart

- Annual budget

- Current financial statements

- Strategic plan

- Recent board meeting minutes

- Committee descriptions

- Key dates

- FAQs about the mission, organization, and programs (including clients and impact)

The handbook should be utilized as a training tool to review information with the new member:

- The treasurer would review financial statements (this would include training on how to interpret them)

- The secretary may review articles of incorporation and bylaws

- The board chair or CEO may be charged with reviewing key timelines, the budget, and the strategic plan

Additionally, the new member should meet with each committee chair to determine where they can best serve.

THE CRITICAL ROLE OF BOARD GOVERNANCE

The role of the governance committee is to ensure board members are recruited, trained, and managed according to the board bylaws. The committee is responsible for board evaluation and serves as an accountability mechanism to address board member noncompliance. A formal evaluation process:

- Provides the opportunity to reflect on performance toward board responsibilities

- Increases board effectiveness

- Builds trust, respect, transparency, and open communication

- Clarifies staff and board roles, expectations, and delineation of responsibilities

- Identifies strengths and opportunities for greater engagement

- Sends the message that the board's role is vital to the success of the organization

At WISE, we recommend having dashboard reports that reflect success metrics for the organization, overall board, and individual board members. An individual member report can be provided privately to them at each board meeting. It should include metrics such as the following:

- Meeting attendance

- Active engagement with a committee

- Introductions to prospective donors, volunteers, and board members

- Personal giving

- Involvement in fundraising events or activities

- Involvement in program activities

WISE RESOURCES

BoardSource provides nonprofit leaders with an extensive range of tools, resources, and research data to increase board effectiveness and strengthen organizational impact. Check out the BoardSource website for examples and templates, such as a board self-assessment questionnaire. Also, refer to BoardSource for example charters for typical board committees.

In the event you have a board member who is disengaged, the governance committee can use the bylaws, board member job description, and dashboard report to remove them. Using objective accountability tools is a kind and gentle way to release them of the commitments they're not able to make. It is a much easier conversation to have when, together, you can review a list of the individual's responsibilities and the ones they are not meeting: "Bob, can we talk about your challenge to attend meetings regularly? We don't want to lose your involvement and your passion for the mission, but we also understand if this role isn't something you can commit to at this time. The good news is there are many other ways for you to be involved that may better fit your availability."

PRIORITIZE RISK MANAGEMENT

One of a board's most important jobs is to minimize risk for the organization. Risk is defined as exposure to the chances of injury and loss. A *risk management* plan, at a minimum, should cover these areas and their respective policies and procedures:

1. **Human resources.** An employee handbook that outlines organizational policies and a code of conduct (including ethical standards), formal job descriptions, background

checks, employee orientation and training, a performance management system, and documented compensation rates.

2. **Financial.** This includes cash handling, investments, internal financial controls, segregation of duties, *unrelated business income*, donation processing, the types of gifts the organization will or won't accept, and how noncash gifts and donations of stock or e-currency will be handled. Considerations should also include financial reporting systems that allow for a budget versus actual expenses review and management of restricted revenue. If an organization has $250,000 or more in revenue and expenses, a financial audit will manage risk associated with financial management issues.

3. **Fundraising.** This includes the adoption of the *Donor Bill of Rights*,[7] gift acknowledgment guidelines, protection of donor information, and implementation of a dynamic donor database that allows for tracking and analysis of donations.

4. **Safety and security.** This category includes use of facilities for programs, adequate insurance coverage, compliance with inspections, proactive maintenance, use of facilities by others, lease agreements, and use of private homes for events.

5. **Information technology (IT).** IT concerns include the physical security of systems and documents, disaster recovery plans, and internet security and usage.

6. **Transportation.** This includes authorized use of organization-owned vehicles and personal vehicles, driver's license/insurance requirements, vehicle selection criteria and main-

---

7 "The Donor Bill of Rights," afpglobal.org (Association of Fundraising Professionals, January 23, 2019), https://afpglobal.org/donor-bill-rights.

tenance, driver log procedures, inspection compliance, and accident procedures.

7. **Brand.** This category includes logo usage, messaging and approval processes, and procedures for public and media relations.

8. **Intellectual property and confidentiality.** This includes a noncompete clause in an employment contract or severance agreement. This is not as common in nonprofits, but protecting the confidentiality of donor, client, and other proprietary information may require a nondisclosure agreement.

9. **Conflicts of interest.** This is an agreement that covers potential or real conflicts of interest. Ethics violations cause the organization to lose stakeholder trust and place it at a competitive disadvantage.

10. *Whistleblower policy.* Every nonprofit should have a whistleblower policy that protects employees or volunteers who report activities believed to be illegal, unethical, dishonest, or improper.

It is the board's job to ensure that these policies and procedures are in place, not to create them (unless there is no staff). The 990 asks whether a nonprofit has a conflict-of-interest policy, a whistleblower policy, and a process to manage conflicts because organizations with these policies and procedures in place are in a better position to manage their risk. If you cannot check yes on the 990 that you have these in place, your 990 is at a higher risk of being audited.

WISE RESOURCES

A nonprofit's insurance broker, banker, and CPA can be invaluable resources to help with considerations in developing risk management policies and plans. Also, check out the Nonprofit Risk Management Center and the Center for Nonprofit Management for tips and templates.

MORE WAYS TO KEEP YOUR BOARD ENGAGED

Ensure that you have strong board communication processes in place. Some organizations utilize an online board portal to communicate, share current documents, and track individual member engagement. A Dropbox or other file sharing account could also serve as a central point of information sharing.

Be intentional in establishing board culture and building rapport and respect among peers. This culture should reflect an expectation of engagement, transparency, shared vision and goals, mission alignment, celebrating wins, and calling out of problematic behaviors.

An annual retreat gives board members the opportunity to celebrate successes, reassess strategic direction, review bylaws, gain new insights, and focus on areas of improvement. Outside experts can help facilitate discussion and decision-making, along with training on topics like board governance, fundraising, and diversity, equity, and inclusion.

Consider ways to bring easy donor stewardship opportunities and mission connections to board members. Some examples include the following:

1. Donor stewardship

- Bring thank-you cards or appeal letters for members to sign at board meetings

- Sign donor thank-you notes for special occasions and holidays

- Make thank-you calls to donors

- Utilize team/group chat platforms to discuss updates, celebrate special moments, and keep communication going

- Host a board social around events like Giving Tuesday, when they can call or email at that moment for donations or to thank donors

- Provide incentives/competitions for board members to invite their networks to an event or share the donation link

- Gamify fundraising goals by splitting the board into teams that compete to hit their goals

- Have the fundraising committee host a quarterly breakfast/coffee, and invite potential or current donors to meet with the CEO

2. Mission connection

  - Share a video or story

  - Share a client visit/video/voice mail of an impact story

  - Have the program team visit to share a mission moment

  - Host board meetings on-site for members to see the mission in action

Staff-Board Overlap and Board Compensation

Occasionally, organizations have staff-board overlap, in which staff members are serving as voting board members or the board chair is also serving as the CEO. In the nonprofit structure, staff report to the executive director (or a similar title, such as president or CEO—these are all basically the same position) who, in turn, reports to the board. The very nature of an employee serving as a governing board member is a conflict of interest, as they cannot report to the executive director (or be the executive director) while holding the executive director (or themselves) accountable for their job performance responsibilities.

This kind of situation can trigger the IRS to conduct an audit or impose immediate sanctions (fines, taxes). Compensation of board members must be divulged on the 990, Part VI, Section A. Leaving this section blank with the argument that the individual is being compensated for their employment and not board service is crossing an ethical boundary because you have individuals serving on the board who are financially compensated by the organization.[8]

While this governance structure is not technically illegal, there are other important risk factors to consider, including the organization's credibility, reputation, and funding. The 990 is reviewed carefully by funders, and most will consider this situation to be a conflict of interest.

In general, it is highly unusual to provide compensation to board members.[9] Sometimes organizations in the start-up or recovery phase have board members filling staff positions or duties without pay. If the

---

8   See specific guidance from the IRS at https://www.irs.gov/pub/irs-tege/governance_practices.pdf.

9   According to the 2017 BoardSource Governance Index, 99 percent of boards surveyed do not financially compensate board members (not even with an honorarium).

organization formally hires a board member in a paid capacity, that member should immediately resign their board position.

WISE PRO TIP: CHANGE MANAGEMENT SHOULD BE PEER LED

Board development work may require change management. Peer-led change will be more successful than CEO- or consultant-led change. Create a well-developed plan for the change using data to support your initiative. Next, consider two or three board members you believe will support your initiative and whose opinion other board members value. Share your plan with those members first. This isn't intended to pressure them to agree; it is to get their feedback. It is also a good idea to float your ideas by the most opinionated and vocal of the board members so that they can poke holes through them and ultimately help you strengthen the plan and become an advocate of it. Once two or three members are in agreement, they are in a position to make an informed presentation to the board and lead the change as peers.

> **Peer-led change will be more successful than CEO– or consultant–led change.**

Word to the WISE

Take a look at your board recruitment and onboarding processes and procedures as well as the accountability tools in place to determine whether they reflect the value of the role and your mission. If not, recruit board members to lead changes needed to create a more effective and engaged board.

CHAPTER

5

PITFALL **5**

You Are Undervaluing Your Organization

In this chapter, we will talk about the ways in which you may be undervaluing your organization, including how that relates to the recruitment of volunteers, staff, and donors. Those working in the nonprofit sector are often reluctant to *impose* upon others by asking them to give of their time, treasure, and talent. Here's the thing: providing people with the *opportunity* to make an informed decision for themselves is not an imposition. Truth is, people want to give, and the number one reason they don't is because they weren't asked.

This *imposition* mindset is unfortunately firmly entrenched in the nonprofit sector, and it requires a shift from "How are we ever going to find someone to do this?" to "Our mission is valuable, and we need to recruit people who are committed to it."

Your Mission Deserves Committed Volunteers

Early in my career and while I was working on my master's degree, I worked at the Cystic Fibrosis Foundation. There, I managed eight fundraising events per year as the only paid staff member. I would never have been able to pull that off without significant volunteer support. Each of my events had a volunteer committee, and over time I realized that some committees worked well and were very engaged, while others lacked follow-through and seemed to fall apart.

You need to *believe* that you deserve committed volunteers. If you don't believe it, no one else will.

What made volunteers follow through? Answering this question was the premise of my master's degree thesis, and I set out to find the answers. I sent out a large-scale volunteer survey and performed in-depth research from which I developed best practices that our firm still applies to our work today.

First, you need to *believe* that you deserve committed volunteers. If you don't believe it, no one else will. Frequently, I've heard nonprofit leaders soft-pitch opportunities to potential volunteers. This involves giving no job description and downplaying the volunteer's responsibilities. It sounds something like this:

"We would love for you to be the event chair for our gala."

"I'm interested. What do I have to do?"

"It would be great for you to help support the event by recruiting other volunteers or donors, but only if you have time."

or

"We have a job description for the role, but it is a lot to ask so I understand if you can't do it."

or

"I know you are a busy person, so all we would really need is for you to sign some sponsorship letters."

When asking someone to volunteer, resist the temptation to give them an out before they even ask for one! *Your ask is an opportunity,* not *an imposition.*

I often coach nonprofit leaders past this underselling/imposition mindset, which usually produces thoughts like, "This is too much to ask of someone" or "We just don't have volunteers who are willing to give this much." If you can identify with these responses, it means one thing: the problem is your mindset, not anyone else's. There are volunteers in your community giving incredible amounts of time, talent, and passion to nonprofit work. Does your mission deserve less dedication than others? I hope your answer is a resounding *no.*

> **Your ask is an opportunity, not an imposition.**

Demonstrate that you are seeking committed volunteers by providing clear expectations with detailed job descriptions. This write-up should be about two pages and include the following:

- Volunteer title

- Success measures (individual goals and campaign goals)

- Purpose

- Suggested or required activities

- Key dates

- Responsibilities (both theirs and the staff's)

- Whom they report to

- Timeline

- Benefits to volunteering

Armed with this, you can have an honest conversation with your volunteer about the expectations of the role. If your volunteer indicates they cannot handle the level of responsibility required, that is OK. It's better to know someone isn't all in now rather than two months before your big event. But don't close the door just yet. Ask them how they can be involved in a way that meets their interests and capacity. Can they take on part of the role and ask a friend to help with the rest? This should be an open and forthright conversation. The key is to never settle for less than what you need—and your mission deserves. If this volunteer isn't the right fit, someone else will be.

GETTING IT WISE: BUILDING YOUR EVENT DREAM TEAM

We recently had a client who was not sold on the value of event committees and was very doubtful when we explained the importance of using a detailed job description to recruit a committee chair. She stuck with us, though, and let us show her the magic of event committees. We helped her identify the ideal committee chair and went along with her to make the ask. To the client's surprise and delight, the volunteer responded with enthusiasm and started talking about others she wanted to ask to join the committee.

In the end, the committee, comprised of megavolunteers who were focused on a fundraising goal, felt so connected to each other and to the organization's mission that the event raised more money than ever before. They even had friendly competitions within the group—who could sell the most sponsorships and who invited the most attendees—and each member genuinely supported the others. Because everyone enjoyed the experience so much, the volunteers' commitment and love of the mission expanded. And when they shared this love with more people who then shared their love … you get the idea.

Now that you understand your organization deserves committed volunteers and you have clear job descriptions for each of them, you can build your event dream team.

RECRUIT STRATEGICALLY

First, recruit your committee chair. Ideally, this would be done with existing committee volunteers and a succession plan so that you could announce the chair for both this year and next. If you cannot recruit your chair from your current committee, consider asking previous chairs or your board members to help you recruit someone.

Once this role has been filled, help them develop a recruitment plan by providing them with job descriptions for key subcommittee positions (logistics, decorations, volunteers, etc.).

Here, you have the opportunity to ask the chair if they have friends, neighbors, and colleagues who might have a passion for the mission and the skills for the positions you are seeking to fill. The more people your chair can personally bring to the committee, the better the chances of building a cohesive team that enjoys working together.

EVERYONE IS COMMITTED TO THE GOAL

It's all about setting and managing expectations. All committee members need to be dedicated to the fundraising goals and should expect to make a financial contribution to the event through sponsorship or another form of donation. All members should be required to sell raffle tickets and sponsorships or *solicit* auction items, as appropriate. Committee success equals event success.

MEET IN PERSON

Meeting regularly and in person keeps the momentum going for the event, holds each member accountable for their tasks, and creates a greater sense of teamwork and rapport among the committee members. Consider making the meetings fun and incorporate a mission moment so that members are excited to attend.

PROMOTE PEER ACCOUNTABILITY

While the event's project manager may be a paid staff member, it is important that the committee is peer led. This means the event chair leads the meetings and holds committee members accountable to their job description and goals as well as associated action items and deliverables. The level of support needed by the committee chair will vary based on their experience, skills, and comfort level in managing their peers. Prepare them to lead meetings by providing an agenda and talking points as needed. Make it clear to the chair which decisions the committee has responsibility for and which ones they do not.

Staff members who are ultimately responsible for the fundraising goal cannot scapegoat volunteers if it isn't reached, so maintaining involvement and providing direction in close partnership with the committee chair is a must. But even this should only go so far. When a staff member leads meetings or holds committee members account-able without going through the chair, they are unlikely to have the same level of success and overall responsiveness as when those efforts are led by the chair.

Your Mission Deserves Qualified Staff

Just like with recruiting volunteers, you want to hire high-level talent for your mission. We frequently encounter boards of directors who believe people who work at nonprofits are self-sacrificing and that serving a mission offsets low wages. Here's the thing: no one can pay their bills with altruism. Everyone wants to be valued for their work, *and* everyone deserves to be paid a fair, livable wage.

Another faulty mindset I've seen is the belief that those who seek higher pay in their nonprofit jobs don't have the same heart and passion for the mission as someone who is willing to accept less. That's simply not true. Nonprofit orga-nizations are no different from any other business in that they require competitive compensation to attract talent. And if you want the best, you must be willing to pay for it.

> No one can pay their bills with altruism. Everyone wants to be valued for their work, and everyone deserves to be paid a fair, livable wage.

A common rationale for keeping salaries low is that *nonprofits need to spare every dollar to serve the mission.* While this is understandable, the fact is that the greatest resource you have in serving your mission are your employees. That requires an investment in attracting and maintaining the best staff out there. Remember Holly's Haven and its cycle of constant turnover? Low salaries led to hiring inexperienced staff who required significant training and were ready to leave once they received the experience needed to make more money elsewhere. This forced the organization's leadership to perpetually spend its time on recruiting and training new staff instead of on strategy, mission impact, and generating resources.

When the board of directors of Holly's Haven decided to hire a new executive director, its board chair called me to discuss an appropriate salary range for the position. He said their market research showed a $65,000 annual salary was suitable based on the size of the organization. While his market research may have been accurate, I explained that they needed to make a decision: if they wanted to keep the organization as it was (barely surviving), they should hire someone at $65,000. That person would likely be someone without executive director experience and who, eventually, would leverage their experience at Holly's Haven for a bigger paycheck elsewhere. But if they really wanted to attract the talent required to rebuild and create a sustainable future, they needed to stretch their budget.

GETTING IT WISE: ATTRACTING QUALIFIED STAFF

At WISE, when we post a position online, we post the minimum starting salary, but not the maximum. This is intentional to encourage equitable salaries. When Focus Texas hired us to recruit their senior fundraising professional, we knew that their chosen salary range for the position was not likely to get them the experienced professional they needed to serve as the organization's fundraising strategist. Leaving the salary range open and asking for salary requirements gave us the opportunity to present Focus Texas with candidates who required salaries within their range as well as candidates who were requesting salaries above their range. Ultimately this strategy caused them to increase their budget to hire someone who could take their fundraising efforts to a new level.

Hiring the best means setting yourself up to hire the best. WISE specializes in recruiting executive-level nonprofit staff, particularly in fundraising, and I'm going to share the secret of our recruitment strategy with you.

TRANSPARENCY IS A MUST

When we take on a recruitment project for a fundraising professional or executive director, we conduct a fundraising assessment. This enables us to envision the ideal candidate and helps us mitigate another contributing factor to high turnover—lack of transparency during the interview process.

With few exceptions, I don't believe that hiring managers intentionally act with a lack of transparency. They just may not know what to share with an interested candidate. They could also be in denial about what is going on within the organization. When it comes down to it, does anyone really want to reveal the negative when they are trying to attract a great candidate? But honesty during an interview—no matter how uncomfortable—is necessary.

As an outside party bringing "third-party self-awareness," we know what candidates need to know, and we share this information with them so they can make an informed decision on whether the position is right for them. Then when they start, they can successfully (and excitedly) hit the ground running—and without feeling blindsided. When we place someone and they come back to us six months later saying they felt prepared to take on the challenges they faced, we know we did our job well.

When vetting candidates, we focus on three qualities as equally important considerations:

1. SKILLS FIT

Even if people may have held positions with titles like **development director** or **event manager**, specific skill sets or experience are not always guaranteed. Many different types of fundraising skills exist, including ones related to special events, **corporate solicitation**, grant writing, and **major gifts solicitation**.

Typically, major gift cultivation requires a different set of skills than writing grants. That said, if you don't dive deep enough into a development director's skills by asking very direct questions about their knowledge and expertise, then you may end up hiring a grant writer when you really need someone who can cultivate major gifts from individuals. And while fundraising skill sets can be transferable across different types of fundraising, grant writing and major gift work require two different personality types.

Grant writing is often an internal-facing fundraising activity. People who like grant writing tend to be introverted and like working in the office, in the quiet space of writing. People who gravitate to major gift work are usually extroverted and love being out in the community meeting people. It's not that you can't find a fundraising unicorn who is good at both activities, but people tend to naturally gravitate toward their comfort zone. And if you are going to err on one side over the other, hire someone with outward-facing fundraising skills for your senior development position since grant writing can easily be outsourced.

2. EXPERIENCE FIT

WISE also looks closely at experience fit. For example, working in a small grassroots nonprofit is different from working in a highly resourced fundraising shop at a university or hospital. So, when you are reviewing a résumé and the job candidate has raised $10 million for a hospital foundation, that doesn't mean they'll be able to do the same for your much smaller organization. It's also important for you to look at the mission for which the candidate had been previously fundraising. Does it align with yours? Did they have the advantage of a built-in audience in their previous role (like alumni or grateful patients)? If so, you'll want to ask questions about whether they are able to start relationships from scratch as well as educate those new prospects on your mission.

3. PERSONALITY FIT

Finally, we consider the fit of a candidate's personality to be just as important as those of skills and experience. We delve in to get a sense of the supervisor's leadership style, along with the leadership needs of the individuals the person will manage.

Some time ago, we were recruiting for a **chief development officer** for an organization that had extremely high turnover in both this role and its overall development department. After interviewing the CEO and the development department staff during the fundraising assessment phase of our process, I quickly picked up on a couple of interesting aspects of the CEO's leadership style: she was a micromanager who had very strong opinions about fundraising strategy, and she believed she was a good coach for individuals who were inexperienced in fundraising but had "potential."

The reality, however, was that she was *not* good at coaching these types of individuals, and she kept getting angry at them for not knowing how to do a job she thought was obvious. As you can imagine, this was a recipe for high turnover.

It is not uncommon for hiring managers to lack self-awareness in this way. This is why it can be helpful to have an outside party, like WISE, evaluate the situation; we can apply what we like to call "third-party self-awareness" to the recruitment process and point out things about leadership style or a work situation that they just don't see.

For this client, we were able to use our recruitment strategy to help them hire someone who stayed four times longer than the historical average for this position.

Your Mission Deserves Donations

You care a great deal about your organization and are committed to its success. Why not give others the chance to care about it as much as you do? That's what fundraising is—providing others an opportunity to invest in something that matters to them.

Let's use a metaphor I think you will relate to. Let's say a restaurant recently opened in your neighborhood, and it's terrific! You eat there frequently enough that you've gotten to know the owner. You want this restaurant to last for the long haul. So what do you do? You start checking in and posting pictures of its delicious dishes on social media. You invite and encourage your friends to eat there. You put in the effort to help it be successful.

Are you less likely to do this for the nonprofit you support?

If you support a mission with great enthusiasm and passion, consider the favor you'd be doing when you introduce it to friends and give them the chance to love it as much as you do. You are a hero all the way around—bringing great opportunities to your friends.

A WISE CAUTIONARY TALE: DON'T STEAL SOMEONE'S OPPORTUNITY

Early in my fundraising career, I was putting on my very first golf tournament in Oklahoma City for the Cystic Fibrosis Foundation. It was at a very exclusive golf course, and the owners allowed only two nonprofit tournaments per year. Entry fees were $500 per player (in this market in the early 2000s, that was an expensive single-player fee). Being the savvy fundraiser (and golfer) I was, I invited everyone I knew who loved golf …

Oh, wait. No, I didn't. *[Record scratch]*

The truth is, I did *not* ask a single friend. Not even the serious golfers. I didn't ask because I was concerned they would feel obligated to participate because of our friendship. *Does that sound familiar?*

In the end, the Swing Fore a Cure Golf Classic was a great success, and we were excited to have it featured in the local newspaper. And *that* was how my friends found out about it. One of them was not happy. He called me immediately. "I can't believe you didn't invite me to this tournament," Trey said. "You know how much I love golf, and this was an exclusive club I never have the chance to play at!"

To say I was embarrassed is an understatement. All I could do was apologize profusely. As I hung up the phone, I had an aha moment. When I didn't invite my friend, I decided "no" on his behalf. *I took away his opportunity. And seriously, how cavalier is that?*

> When I didn't invite my friend, I decided "no" on his behalf. I took away his opportunity.

One reason people participate in fundraising events like the Swing Fore a Cure Golf Classic is to gain access to a social group or another group of decision makers. The Classic was chaired by an independent oil and gas producer whose family was impacted by the mission. When he invited his peers and vendors, it became an industry event, and I sold it as such. In considering additional sponsors, I thought about those businesses that would like to have access to these decision makers, such as benefit service providers and financial institutions. Individuals who network at events like this are gaining social capital. Trey is a financial planner, so withholding the opportunity to participate in the Classic was a disservice to him from a social capital perspective as well.

Donors Give to Meet Their Needs

Everyone has their own reasons why they're involved with a nonprofit. For some, donating to an organization may provide them the recognition they seek from a social group. Some want to leave a legacy, while others are drawn to an organization's impact. You won't know someone's motivation to get involved unless you ask. The more informed you are, the better you can determine how a gift to your organization may meet their needs.

When I worked for the American Heart Association in the mid-2000s, I was trained not to bring sponsorship packets to meetings with potential corporate sponsors. The first meeting is not about asking for a donation, it's an opportunity to ask questions about the company:

- Who's your target audience? Tell me about your marketing goals.

- What do you like about your current sponsorship relationships with nonprofits?

- What criteria do you use when deciding about partnering with a nonprofit?

- What's your budget cycle? When do you make sponsorship decisions?

The key is to ask and listen. Then come back to them with a thoughtful, customized sponsorship proposal with options that meet their needs. This is called needs-based selling, and it works. You just need three magical skills: curiosity, active listening, and the ability to creatively connect with someone's interests.

An appropriate ask is the intersection of what you believe your organization is worthy of requesting and what you understand to be the donor's desires and ability to give. Now, if you don't believe your organization is worthy of a $10,000 donation, then you shouldn't request it. But ask yourself why. Is it because you need to shift your mindset, or because your nonprofit lacks the service delivery or impact? Assess the problem and then solve it.

Word to the WISE

*If you don't have confidence in the value of your
mission, you can't expect anyone else to.*

Spend some time reflecting on your mindset about how you sell your mission to others—does it reflect your passion and belief in its value?

CHAPTER 6

PITFALL **6**

You Are Not Fully Living Your Mission

Over the past five chapters, we have covered how the function of your operations, programs and fundraising impacts your sustainability (the three-legged stool metaphor); how your financials are telling a story; how to develop an engaged board; how to ensure your organization is financially sustainable; and how to avoid undervaluing your mission. In this chapter, we'll discuss what it looks like to have your actions truly reflect your love for your mission.

Building a Culture of Philanthropy

I'm sure you've heard the buzz phrase *"culture of philanthropy,"* but what does it mean? And more importantly, what does it look like in practice?

Creating a culture of philanthropy is a self-reflective process that involves asking questions and developing a commitment to philanthropy's role in your mission. Consider the following questions:

DOES YOUR ORGANIZATION'S LEADERSHIP UNDERSTAND THE IMPORTANCE OF PHILANTHROPY?

In our fundraising assessment of a large, statewide nonprofit, Focus Texas, we recommended that its leadership intentionally implement a culture of philanthropy. The CEO acknowledged this was a need and recognized that because the organization's programs were primarily funded by government contracts, they had become complacent about fundraising activities and diversifying revenue. As discussed in chapter 3, this type of reliance on government funding can create serious sustainability issues.

Further, when it came to Focus Texas's board of directors, not all members were contributing financially to the organization. Most didn't help with fundraising efforts, as they didn't really see the need. Focus Texas's leadership had to shift from raising the minimum **contributed revenue** needed to survive to diversifying revenue for long-term thriving. Changing a mindset must start at the top. Let's break this down.

An established culture of philanthropy means that every year, every board member makes a personal financial gift. Note the key words "personal" and "financial." This is not the same as a board member getting their employer to sponsor an event or a member donating their mileage reimbursement back to the organization. They should already be doing these things. A personal financial gift is a *cash* gift.

The expectation to give should be formal and outlined in the board's bylaws—often referred to as a give-get policy. Some even stipulate a minimum gift amount.

If it's not specified, it should be a gift that is meaningful to the board member. This, however, looks different for everyone. And that's OK. It's not the size of the gift that matters.

Why are these gifts so important? Because if your board—the senior leadership of the organization—doesn't believe enough in the mission to financially support it, how can they expect others to do so?

> If your board—the senior leadership of the organization—doesn't believe enough in the mission to financially support it, how can they expect others to do so?

For Focus Texas, we helped them implement a give-get policy by helping them identify board members to serve on a **development committee.** This group drives the process of establishing the policy, as well as ensures compliance with it. The process of establishing the committee and policies should be peer led.

WISE PRO TIP: EQUIP A BOARD TO FUNDRAISE

If you have board members who make excuses about why they cannot fundraise, like they need more training or a pitch deck, it can be an indication that they are just not comfortable with fundraising and will make excuses until the end of time. Fundraising is a conversation and does not require a fancy pitch deck. However, I always recommend that you check the usual excuse boxes (like training and a visual aid that they can refer to). Then you'll know whether they have any intention of talking to others about the value of your mission.

When working with a board that is newly embracing a culture of philanthropy, we often provide a Fundraising 101 training that covers an overview of giving, donor motivations, and how to see fundraising as a way of giving others an opportunity to meet their personal needs as a donor. We encourage board members to think about the different ways they can support fundraising efforts, whether it is making thank-you calls or writing thank-you notes, leveraging their social networks, or asking friends to join them on their next volunteer activity. Most people can connect with fundraising in a way that makes sense for them.

HOW ARE YOU MINIMIZING THE FUNDRAISING FUNCTION IN YOUR ORGANIZATION?

Our next project with Focus Texas was to recruit its senior fundraiser. While the CEO understood the need to raise additional funds and implement a culture of philanthropy, the importance of fundraising as an essential function of the mission was not reflective in the *organizational chart*. She had titled all members of her *executive team* as vice presidents—except her senior fundraiser, who was titled as a director and reported to a VP of strategy rather than directly to the CEO. Without realizing it, she was minimizing the fundraising function within the organization.

When we pointed out that the senior fundraiser should have direct access to the CEO and influence on organizational strategy with a seat on the executive team, her mindset began to shift. In the end, she elevated this position and hired an experienced professional (who ultimately became her successor) to take the organization's fundraising to the next level. Appropriately positioning this function in your organization not only emphasizes its role in serving your mission but also gives you the opportunity to attract the best talent.

HOW DOES YOUR LEADERSHIP TALK ABOUT FUNDRAISING?

Now let's reflect more deeply on how having a culture of philanthropy is fully living your mission. Here are some common phrases nonprofit leaders say, what they really mean, and what they should be saying instead:

STATEMENT: "I can talk about the organization, but I can't ask for money."

SOUNDS LIKE: "I can't make a case for why someone should support this."

TRY: "I believe in the value of our mission, and I'm excited to tell others about why they should support it."

STATEMENT: "I'm too busy with the actual mission work to fundraise."

SOUNDS LIKE: "Fundraising doesn't contribute to our mission."

TRY: "Fundraising is essential to our mission."

STATEMENT: "I'm not a salesperson."

SOUNDS LIKE: "Philanthropy is a disingenuous transaction."

TRY: "We are building relationships with donors who are invested in our mission."

STATEMENT: "I hate fundraising."

SOUNDS LIKE: "Fundraising is bad."

TRY: "I am thankful for the philanthropy that makes our mission work possible."

Consider that last statement: "I hate fundraising." I've heard this like a mantra from others throughout my entire career. Nonprofit volunteers and staff at all levels say this without thinking about how diminishing it is. If you believe that what you put out into the world comes back to you, then an organization with this message is conveying that fundraising, and its role in serving the mission, is not valued.

All these statements tell the listener that the mission isn't worthy of investment, but this last one in particular tells the fundraisers in your organization that they are not a valuable contributor to the mission.

What if individuals connected with your organization said, "I hate programs," with such ease?

IS YOUR BOARD TREATING YOUR PROGRAMS AND FUNDRAISING FUNCTIONS EQUALLY?

At board meetings, it's not uncommon to see a chief development officer reporting on progress toward their goals. This burden of proving success, however, is not always placed on the **chief programs officer**. Boards often do not demand progress reports on programmatic success the way they do with fundraising goals. This results in

108

less access, involvement, and understanding between the board and programs staff. Of course, this can be flipped, and the fundraising function can have less access or burden of proving success. Either way, it is important to treat these functions as equally important to the success of your mission.

IS YOUR FUNDRAISER AT THE RIGHT TABLES?

Are you inviting to the table those who will be seeking funding for a new program at the same time you're developing that program and its messaging? I mentioned in chapter 1 why this is important—fundraisers are the ear of funders and are more likely to have a sense of their perspective. Even if you are a small organization and do not have professional fundraising staff, make sure there is a "mental seat at the table," at the very least. Organizations and their programs are only as viable as they are fundable.

HOW ARE YOU MESSAGING THE IMPORTANCE OF PHILANTHROPY TO YOUR CLIENTS?

When you talk about your services, do you tell clients they're free? *"Free"* takes the face away from the gift. When I was the national director of field fundraising at Mothers Against Drunk Driving (MADD), I worked hard to change the narrative from "Victim services are free" to "Victim services are provided at no cost to victims, thanks to the generosity of our donors." This second version tells the recipient: "Someone gifted this to you."

St. Jude Children's Research Hospital does this very well. Families never receive an invoice for treatment, and St. Jude also covers travel expenses. It explains to its patients' families that unlike other hospitals, most of its funding comes from generous donors. By acknowledging this generosity, the recipients of those services are more likely to pay it forward when they are in a position to do so.

While this distinction seems subtle, it really is living your mission to the fullest and recognizing that generosity makes the mission possible. It is taking the love of your mission full circle.

ARE YOU PROVIDING GREAT "CUSTOMER SERVICE"?

By keeping a strong focus on best practices of customer service, you can create a positive experience for every person who engages with your organization. Here are ways to do so:

- Answer the phone with a smile and a welcoming tone every time

- Respond to board, donor, and volunteer emails and phone calls, as well as social media comments and messages, within twenty-four hours

- Keep your website up to date and responsive to mobile devices

- Personalize your communications with a name

- Make it easy for people to donate on your website

- Cultivate the mindset that all staff share responsibility for engaging donors and volunteers

ARE YOU CREATING A SUPPORTIVE ENVIRONMENT FOR YOUR FUNDRAISING TEAM?

Before I started consulting, I managed the fundraising department at a large statewide organization. Our programs, which were funded primarily by government grants, were consistently out of compliance with the funder's requirements. Government grants are usually *reimbursement grants*, which means that you spend the money first, then prove that you spent the money according to the funder's requirements. So when our programs were not in compliance, we weren't being reimbursed. This put us in a cash flow crisis.

In the executive team meeting in which we discussed how we were bleeding money because of this noncompliance, I was told the solution: my department needed to raise more money. This was absurd. Our operational and programs legs of our stool were crippled, and the fundraising leg would not be far behind.

Too often, fundraising staff are expected to carry the burden of generating revenue for the organization with minimal or no help from the board, CEO, or other organizational staff. When they are faced with unreasonable expectations, the fundraisers become the scapegoats, or they become burned out. In both situations, they usually leave.

A WISE CAUTIONARY TALE: A FUNDRAISING PROFESSIONAL IS NOT A SOLO CRUSADER

As I am writing, we are in the midst of what has become known as the Great Resignation, a ripple effect of shifting priorities caused by the COVID-19 pandemic that has led to employees throughout the country quitting in record numbers. Even before the pandemic, a 2019 article in *Chronicle of Philanthropy* reported that more than half of fundraising professionals surveyed planned to leave their jobs within two years due to too much pressure to meet unrealistic fundraising goals, along with too little pay and frustrating organizational cultures.[10] Worse yet, three out of ten fundraisers surveyed said they planned to leave the nonprofit sector altogether.

Within this climate, we have had to coach several clients in hiring their first fundraising professional. I recently completed a fundraising assessment for Doctors in the Community as part of a project to recruit its first development director. Unfortunately, this assessment revealed that the organization was deficit spending, with barely enough cash and projected revenue to survive the next three months. The board was disinterested in participating in fundraising activities, and only some of them were donors.

Their sentiment was that the newly hired development director would single-handedly bring in the revenue needed to create financial stability. Especially in a hiring market in which experienced fundraisers are in high demand, nonprofits have the burden to demonstrate that they are desirable places to work. That includes providing a supportive environment, reasonable goals, and a culture of philanthropy.

In the case of Doctors in the Community, I explained that their situation would not be likely to attract an experienced fundraising professional. Even if we could find someone to take on the role, perhaps due to a connection to the mission, that person would be quickly overwhelmed by the expectation of saving the organization and have almost no support from a disengaged board. Given the

---

10   Heather Joslyn, "51% Of Fundraisers Plan to Leave Their Jobs by 2021, Says New Survey," philanthropy.com (*The Chronicle of Philanthropy*, August 6, 2019), https://www.philanthropy.com/article/51-of-fundraisers-plan-to-leave-their-jobs-by-2021-says-new-survey/.

predicament, they would likely leave within three months. In the end, our assessment determined that the organization was not ready to hire a fundraising professional.

Instead, it needed to implement an all-hands-on-deck strategy to raise the money needed to keep their doors open.

When everyone becomes actively involved in a culture of philanthropy, the capacity for fundraising and the network are exponentially multiplied.

We've had similar conversations with several other clients. If you do not have a culture of philanthropy that supports fundraising efforts, and you think a new fundraiser will shoulder the burden of generating revenue, you are not ready to hire one. When everyone becomes actively involved in a culture of philanthropy, the capacity for fundraising and the network are exponentially multiplied. Then, with a skilled fundraising professional, the possibilities are endless.

Clients as Donors

Occasionally, I've heard that it is inappropriate to ask a client to give financially to the organization. Let's unpack this.

While I was working at MADD's national office, there was an unofficial policy about not asking the families of victims to donate. The thinking was that they had endured the tragic loss of a loved one, and as such, it was inappropriate to ask them to give financially. In the big picture, however, it was still MADD's mission to prevent these senseless deaths so that others didn't have to experience the same trauma.

During that time, I oversaw the implementation of our largest national fundraising effort, Walk Like MADD. This event relies on participants asking friends and family to donate to support them as they walk to raise awareness for a cause they care deeply about. It's a popular fundraising strategy that sees small donations add up to big dollars. Part of my role was to develop best practices when it came to executing the event and training field staff and volunteers to duplicate it in cities across the country. In this process, I was surprised to start hearing that many of our fundraising professionals were getting pushback from program staff who refused to share certain contact information, specifically that of families who had lost loved ones. This information was to be used to share news about the Walk Like MADD event the organization would soon be hosting in the families' cities. According to the programs staff, they didn't want these families to be burdened by being asked to give financially.

> **Don't close the door for others, regardless of your assumptions about their financial positions, emotional states, or readiness.**

This mindset, however, was denying a simple truth: these families are the people most compelled by MADD's mission. They have powerful, personal reasons to see that it is realized. Most participants in "a-thon" events, like the Komen Race for the Cure˙ and Walk MS, have their own motivations in doing so—they might be battling said disease or issue, are a survivor, or perhaps have lost a loved one to it.

In this situation at MADD, the program staff's efforts to gatekeep contact information, while driven by good intentions, denied families the opportunity to make a decision that could save others from the grief they had endured. Don't close the door for others, regardless of your assumptions about their financial positions, emotional states, or readiness. Sometimes fundraising is one of the only ways people impacted by the mission, and those who love them, can reach out and help.

Volunteers as Donors

To a nonprofit organization, volunteers are the boots on the ground and are often the most invested in the mission. They are the foundation of program services and an integral part of effective fundraising efforts. This is why I have always been amazed by the perception that it is unacceptable to ask a volunteer to make a financial gift. It goes back to these questions:

- Do you believe your organization is worthy of investment?

- Who should decide what level of giving is too much for someone?

- Shouldn't people be trusted to decide for themselves?

WISE REFERENCE

A comprehensive study performed by Fidelity Charitable found that volunteers support their causes with both time and money—not one or the other.[11] Eighty-seven percent of volunteers say there is overlap between the organizations they support financially and where they volunteer, with 43 percent describing a significant or total overlap. While volunteers are more likely (58 percent) to support a

---

11   "Time and Money: The Role of Volunteering in Philanthropy," fidelitycharitable.org (Fidelity Charitable, 2014), https://www.fidelitycharitable.org/content/dam/fc-public/docs/insights/volunteering-and-philanthropy.pdf.

charity financially before volunteering, 42 percent volunteered at a charity before donating to that organization, and 50 percent say volunteering leads them to give more financial support.

To live your mission with your volunteers, it is critical to engage them intentionally and strategically. Two key components of this are understanding a volunteer's motivation and providing meaningful opportunities. As when donating funds, people give their time for a variety of reasons. They may get involved because they want to make an impact on a mission they care about, someone they care about asked them to, they want to acquire new skills, or perhaps they seek recognition within a social group.

To live your mission with your volunteers, it is critical to engage them intentionally and strategically.

Whatever is driving them, find out by asking. Ask why they got involved, which program interests them most, and what other ways they may want to engage with your mission. Don't let their responses fall into the void—act upon them by using this information to communicate intentionally. In doing so, you will be able to provide the meaningful opportunity they are looking for.

Living your mission with your volunteers means reflecting their value through your actions. One way to do this is to invest in systems that make volunteering easy for them. A nonprofit that has more than fifty active volunteers or is hosting volunteer group projects should have a dedicated volunteer coordinator or manager on staff. Small organizations can get away with having a joint volunteer or development coordinator until greater capacity is achieved. The role of this person is to oversee the recruitment, training, and retention of volunteers.

Demonstrate the value of and respect for a volunteer's role by providing job descriptions, ongoing training, and regular performance check-ins. These tell individuals their volunteer job is important, demands accountability, and reflects that you are willing to invest in them.

WISE PRO TIP: USE ONE CRM FOR ALL CONSTITUENTS

You also need to invest in your volunteer manager. Whether they are paid or not, your volunteer manager will need resources to get the job done. CRM software is the hub of all volunteer data for demographics, volunteer roles, level of activity, scheduling, and communication.

I recommend that your CRM includes all appropriate constituents, including your clients and volunteers—who, remember, are also potential donors. You want to make sure you are not leaving anyone out when communicating about your organization, sharing volunteer opportunities, and extending invitations to support your mission financially. Having constituents in different databases instead of one CRM can lead to duplicating data and then cumbersome *deduping* of contact information when you are prepping to send a communication piece.

It's also important to show your appreciation for your volunteers. For inspiration, check out a blog post on our website in which fellow consultants Suzanne Smith of Social Impact Architects and Aimee Sheahan of Sheahan Communications and I share how to "show love" to the VIPs of nonprofits. Using Dr. Gary Chapman's *The 5 Love Languages* as a guide, we put our own twist on words of affirmation, acts of service, receiving gifts, quality time, and physical touch.

Word to the WISE

Avoid the pitfall of not fully living your mission by understanding the essential role of philanthropy in serving it. Take stock of how your organization is valuing fundraising within your organization and giving others an opportunity to support your worthy mission.

PITFALL  **7**

The Calls Are Coming from Inside the House

Could your staff be a client of one of your programs?

While serving others, we often lose sight of ourselves. We are so busy feeding our neighbors that we don't even realize our family is starving within our own home. This happens in our daily lives as individuals, and it happens on a large organizational scale in nonprofits. Are we, in essence, pointing at the world, saying it needs help, while ignoring the fingers pointing back at ourselves to remind us that we do too?

Throughout this book, I have challenged you to confront the most common pitfalls that I have seen during my nonprofit career, and this may be one of the costliest to your organization's well-being. In this chapter, we'll look at two of the most important ways nonprofits can fail their employees: underpaying them and not caring for trauma.

Everyone Deserves Financial Stability

Remember Holly's Haven from chapter 1? It was operating on a shoe-string budget, which translated to low pay for the staff. The result of this lack of equitable compensation? Turnover within the program staff was, on average, every three months. This created an unsustainable cycle in which the executive director had to constantly recruit, onboard, and train new staff.

When a board of directors, often made up of individuals with more than moderate financial means, pays staff salaries or wages that are under market value compared to similar for-profit roles, it reflects a misalignment of perceived employee motivation and value of the role.

It is a commonly held belief that those who get into nonprofit work are not motivated by money—or to be more precise, *should not* be motivated by money. After all, the whole point of nonprofits is altruism, right? If I had a dime for every time I heard someone say something like, "Well, you didn't get into nonprofits because you care about money," I would have enough dimes to launch a nonprofit!

> Everyone wants and deserves financial security and to be able to support themselves and their families, just like everyone wants to be compensated fairly for their efforts.

I don't believe it is greedy to care about your income. Everyone wants and deserves financial security and to be able to support themselves and their families, just like everyone wants to be compensated fairly for their efforts. It is true that most nonprofit professionals choose this line of work because they are motivated by finding meaning in how they spend their day. But when a board of directors believes that "feeling good" makes up for low compensation, it is doing a disservice to the organization's employees and to the mission itself.

Not only do many nonprofits provide a subpar salary, but they also often expect employees to work more than forty hours in a week. Even further, many nonprofits violate employment law by asking employees to volunteer for activities above and beyond their paid work hours. It is *illegal* to allow a nonexempt (hourly) employee to volunteer to work unpaid for events or other employer-related activities. Nonexempt employees must be paid for *all* time worked. On the flip side, some nonprofits protect the time of nonexempt employees and take advantage of exempt ones.

According to Glassdoor, the median salary for a US nonprofit worker is $55,462, just a little over the national average cost of living, which is $53,329,[12] leaving virtually no room for building assets, taking vacations, or making charitable donations.

In early 2016, the US Department of Labor finalized the most significant update to federal rules on overtime in decades, more than doubling the salary threshold for guaranteed overtime pay from about $23,000 to $47,476 ($22.83/hour). It requires employers to pay overtime at a rate of at least time and one-half the employee's regular rate for each hour they work over forty in a workweek. This means that if an employee making $47,476 works five hours of overtime per week for fifty-two weeks, they would earn an additional $9,293 of pay in a year ($35.74/hour for each hour over forty hours worked in a week).

---

12   "Salary: Non Profit (April, 2023)," glassdoor.com (Glassdoor, 2023), https://www.glassdoor.com/Salaries/non-profit-salary-SRCH_KO0,10. htm#:~:text=%2455%5C2C,770,-%2F%20yr&text=How%20accurate%20does%20 %2455%5C2C770%20look%20to%20you%3F&text=Your%20input%20helps%20 Glassdoor%20refine%20our%20pay%20estimates%20over%20time.

Unsurprisingly, this change fueled pushback from large corporations, but resistance from one organization was surprising to many.
In a statement opposing the change, Public Interest Research Group
(PIRG), a progressive nonprofit and self-proclaimed advocate for the
public interest ("We speak out for the public and stand up to special
interests on problems that affect the public's health, safety and well-
being"), contended that "doubling the minimum salary to $47,476
is especially unrealistic for nonprofit, cause-oriented organizations.
[T]o cover higher staffing costs forced upon us under the rule, we
will be forced to hire fewer staff and limit the hours those staff can
work—all while the well-funded special interests that we're up against
will simply spend more."[13]

Habitat for Humanity was one of the national nonprofits that
agreed with PIRG's assessment with a public statement: "Because
nonprofit charitable organizations pay employees less, on average,
than for-profit businesses, the proposed changes will disproportion-
ately impact their budgets. *The salary for the majority of Habitat affiliates' CEOs or executive directors, the highest paid affiliate employee, is less
than the [salary threshold that would] be required for exemption under
the proposed rule and far less than CEO's working in the for profit sector.*
(Emphasis mine.)"[14] It asserted that the nearly $27,000 increase in
the minimum salary to qualify for the overtime exemption represents
one-third to one-quarter of the cost of building a typical Habitat
home. And further explained that for a smaller, rural affiliate "that
works tirelessly" to raise enough funds to build just one house each
year, it may be impossible to absorb the increased cost of paying

---

13   "Statement on the Overtime Rule," pirg.org (Public Interest Research Group, May 18,
      2016), https://pirg.org/media-center/statement-on-the-overtime-rule/.

14   Christopher Ptomey. letter to Ms. Mary Ziegler, "Re: Defining and Delimiting the
      Exemptions for Executive, Administrative, Professional, Outside Sales and Computer
      Employees," Washington, DC: 200 Constitution Avenue NW, September 4, 2015.

overtime, causing the affiliate to cease operations even if it is the only affordable housing provider in the community. The statement further asserted that "Exemption requirements must carefully *balance the income needs of employees of charitable organizations with the community needs served by such organizations.* (Emphasis mine.)"[15]

In essence, PIRG and Habitat for Humanity were demanding the right to stand on the backs of underpaid employees, many of whom could possibly be clients, in the name of service to the community.

RIGHTSIZE SALARIES

To rightsize your organization's salaries, conduct a salary audit and comparison. If you don't have an HR department to handle it, an HR consultant can help. You'll want to make sure that you are analyzing your organization's salaries in comparison to similar nonprofit roles at organizations of similar sizes. Then take it a step further, and compare them to similar for-profit roles.

Next consider the future of your organization: Where do you want to be in two years? Five years? Ten years? Then look at the salaries of similar positions in that size organization.

Remember in the last chapter, when Holly's Haven's board chair asked me about a reasonable salary for their executive director position? I explained to him that if they wanted to stay small, they should pay a comparable salary for an agency their size, or they could stretch their budget to get the experience they needed to stabilize and grow. Know where you want to be within the next few years and what it will cost for you to pay salaries at that level.

Finally, make sure that you are comparing salaries *within* your nonprofit to ensure that you are creating equitable salary bands at each

---

15   Ibid.

level of the organizational chart. Nonprofits tend to pay higher salaries for development staff than program staff. Make sure that you have an established salary range for each level of position in your organization and that you are not skewing salaries to favor one department over another. If you end up hiring someone at a director level who demands a significantly higher salary than your other directors, it's time to look at a salary adjustment for your other directors. It may also be an indication that it's time for you to do an organizational salary audit.

I know it is not realistic to think that a nonprofit can just change the salary structure and implement it overnight. It relies on funding. Once you have determined your new salary targets, make an implementation plan. You may have to implement it incrementally over the next one to three years. You can also create a tiered budget (refer back to chapter 3) so that salary increases can be triggered at a specific revenue target. Also, for funders who may question why you are paying higher salaries, be ready to reference your pay analysis, business case, and philosophy on hiring and paying for the talent that your mission deserves.

WISE PRO TIP

It is considered unethical within the fundraising profession to pay or receive a percentage of funds raised to a consultant or staff member. Fundraisers who belong to the Association of Fundraising Professionals must commit to the following:[16]

---

16 "Code of Ethical Standards," afpglobal.org (Association of Fundraising Professionals, February 13, 2023), https://afpglobal.org/ethicsmain/code-ethical-standards.

1. Must not accept compensation or enter into a contract that is based on a percentage of contributions; nor shall members accept finder's fees or contingent fees.

2. Must be permitted to accept performance-based compensation, such as bonuses, only if such bonuses are in accord with prevailing practices within the members' own organizations and are not based on a percentage of contributions.

3. Must neither offer nor accept payments or special considerations for the purpose of influencing the selection of products or services.

4. Must not pay finder's fees, commissions, or percentage compensation based on contributions.

5. Must meet the legal requirements for the disbursement of funds if they receive funds on behalf of a donor or client.

Your Staff May Have Experienced Trauma

While compensation is a tangible indicator of how employees are valued, it is not the only way an organization can demonstrate this. In the same way that some might think nonprofit employees committed to a mission should just accept a low wage due to the altruistic nature of their work, staff and volunteers are often expected to put their own pain and stress aside to care for others without adequate support or resources.

Nonprofit workers may witness or hear about traumatic events that take time to process. Because many who work in nonprofits are there because of a shared experience with the people they are serving, these events can trigger one's own personal traumas—bringing them back to the surface and impacting their ability to cope and perform. Even if a worker doesn't have shared experience that drives their commitment to the mission, they may have experienced personal or work-related traumas that they are bringing into their role.

> **Nonprofit workers often bear witness to a tremendous amount of trauma and stress.**

Furthermore, nonprofit workers often bear witness to a tremendous amount of trauma and stress. When an individual repeatedly sees, hears, and takes on the feelings of others' traumatic experiences, how is that individual impacted?

WISE REFERENCE: RECOGNIZING TRAUMA EXPOSURE RESPONSES

The Figley Institute's Compassion Fatigue Educator Guide describes the following types of trauma responses commonly found in caregiver roles:

- Secondary traumatic stress describes the phenomenon whereby individuals become traumatized not by directly experiencing a traumatic event but by hearing about a traumatic event experienced by someone else.

- Vicarious trauma is a negative transformation in the self that results from empathic engagement with traumatized clients and their reports of traumatic experiences, resulting in a disruption of spirituality, meaning, and hope.

- Compassion fatigue refers to the emotional and physical exhaustion that can affect helping professionals and caregivers over time. It has been associated with a gradual desensitization to client stories, a decrease in quality care, an increase in errors, higher rates of depression and anxiety disorders among helpers, and rising rates of time off and degradation in the workplace.[17]

As I see it, trauma stewardship refers to the entire conversation about how we come to do this work, how we are affected by it and how we make sense of and learn from our experiences.
—LAURA VAN DERNOOT LIPSKY

In her book *Trauma Stewardship,* Laura van Dernoot Lipsky, through her personal experiences and those of other caregivers, describes trauma exposure and its impact. The following are just some of the common trauma exposure responses:

1. Feeling helpless and hopeless: Becoming overwhelmed by the feeling that the work you do is insignificant compared to the scale of larger problems, such as inequality or poverty.

2. A sense that one can never do enough: Lacking a sense of accomplishment or success and feeling like no amount of work that you do will ever be enough to alleviate the suffering of others.

3. Diminished creativity: Having less energy to come up with new ideas or ways of understanding that can help solve problems, aid in better communication, or provide an expressive outlet.

---

17   "Basics of Compassion Fatigue," figleyinstitute.com (The Figley Institute, 2012), http://www.figleyinstitute.com/documents/Workbook_AMEDD_ SanAntonio_2012July20_RevAugust2013.pdf.

4. Chronic exhaustion or physical ailments: Experiencing physical and mental exhaustion and illness that go unaddressed and untreated.

5. Sense of persecution: Feeling under the control of the persistence of demands coming from others, which can lead to feeling like you have no control over your work.

6. Anger and cynicism: Building up resentment and an inclination to expect negative outcomes.

7. Inability to empathize or numbing: Repressing the ability to recognize and understand the thoughts or emotions of other people.

8. Grandiosity: Not knowing who you are outside of work.[18]

The last one, grandiosity, reflects the sense of purpose that draws many people to nonprofit work. It can also make them more vulnerable to overidentifying with the work. This is especially true for those who have shared experiences with the individuals they are serving.

WISE RESOURCES

Do any of these trauma exposure responses hit home for you? Or are you recognizing some of these responses in your staff? If the answer is yes, I encourage you to read *Trauma Stewardship* as a first step. Here are some additional books that I recommend to explore more about human responses to stress and trauma:

- *The Body Keeps the Score: Brain, Mind, and Body in the Healing of Trauma*, by Bessel van der Kolk

---

18   Laura van Dernoot Lipsky, *Trauma Stewardship* (Oakland, California: Berrett-Koehler Publishers, 2009).

- *Mindsight: The New Science of Personal Transformation*, by Daniel J. Siegel, MD

- *Anatomy of the Soul: Surprising Connections Between Neuroscience and Spiritual Practices That Can Transform Your Life and Relationships*, by Curt Thompson

Have you asked your staff if they are feeling any symptoms of trauma? If you read through this list and you think, "Nope. Not me," don't forget that everyone has their own experience. Be careful not to assume that your trauma experience, level of resilience, or coping skills are the same as those you work with.

It's also important to remember that nonprofits are often high-pressure environments where employees are overworked and under-resourced. This constant undercurrent of stress can create a hypervigilant state that can feel like trauma. Human beings were designed for survival. Your reptilian brain (think fight, flight, freeze) doesn't know the difference between fear resulting from a lion attack and fear while waiting for the announcement of the fourth round of layoffs. People under a constant state of stress will exist in survival mode—hypervigilance with a diminished ability to focus and process information, acting without thinking, or completely avoiding situations, to the detriment of the work.

It seems like the typical response to someone facing intense stress is to encourage them to do more "self-care." I know what it feels like to live in survival mode under constant stress. While in this state, when people would suggest self-care to me, I would laugh. It always brought an image to my mind of "self-care" as a smaller-than-life-sized person pushing against a herd of stampeding elephants representing everything I felt I had no control over. I laughed at the audacity of the suggestion that I needed to focus more on self-care—I was too overwhelmed to see my way out of the stampede.

Artist: Vanessa Delgado

I challenge you to think beyond encouraging your employees to engage in self-care. Many people (like me when I was in survival mode) have barriers to self-care, often including a lack of awareness of their own trauma responses and what is needed to address them.

Building a Culture That Supports Mental and Emotional Health

As an organization, when you think about your culture, does it reflect your values?

As a leader of a new and growing company, I made a common mistake that many founders do. I just kind of let the corporate culture develop itself. Then when the resulting culture conflicted with our values, changing it became a massive undertaking. My hope is that sharing our journey will help provide a road map for yours.

Step 1: The first step in changing our culture started with sitting down as a leadership team and taking a hard look at how the culture came to be and owning our roles in it.

Step 2: The next step was to reassess our corporate values and what a culture that reflected those values would look like. Our corporate values are strategy (critical thinking), achievement, excellence, integrity, and respect. These values represent our corporate promise and reflect our commitment to our clients. But we needed to take this a step further and vision out our ideal culture. What does upholding these values look like in practice?

At WISE, we are big fans of Patrick Lencioni, author of *The Five Dysfunctions of a Team*, *The Ideal Team Player*, and (a required read for all our employees) *Getting Naked*. In *The Ideal Team Player*, he uses a parable to talk about the three characteristics of the ideal team player—hungry, humble, and smart. We adopted these characteristics as an overarching lens that describes how our values are demonstrated in practice. We interpret these three characteristics—hungry, humble, and smart—to look like this:

- Demonstrating leadership, regardless of title or supervisory authority

- Being a lifelong learner with a commitment to ongoing professional and personal development

- Having a commitment to achievement and drive for success

- Having the ability to adapt a communication style and approach to meet the situation

- Having the ability to synthesize large quantities of information to determine patterns and make recommendations on strategy[19]

Step 3: Then, we had to look at all the systems within the company to determine how they were feeding the culture. We took the framework of hungry, humble, and smart and used it to update our new employee recruitment and onboarding process, our performance management procedures, and even how we evaluate current and potential client relationships (as our clients also contribute to our culture). In each of these systems, we have created clear expectations and accountability tools.

Finally, once we did all this work, we felt like we could describe our culture in two words that would serve as our north stars—caring and feedback. We strive to have a caring culture (in which everyone feels supported) and a feedback culture (in which expectations are always clear). And we believe that people who are hungry, humble, and smart will thrive in a culture that is fueled by strategy, achievement, excellence, integrity, and respect.

This culture defining work took well over a year, and it requires ongoing effort to continually hold ourselves accountable to it. As you reflect on your organization's culture and how it supports the mental and emotional health of your workers, here are some values-based recommendations to consider:

1. **Promote work-life balance.** As a member of the tail end of Generation X, I spent much of my career working insanely long hours in the name of achievement. My kind might be the last of the martyred self-sacrificing ilk. When I was a young professional working hard to prove my worth at a

---

19   Patrick Lencioni, *The Ideal Team Player: How to Recognize and Cultivate the Three Essential Virtues* (Hoboken, New Jersey: Jossey-Bass, 2016).

large national nonprofit, one of the senior leaders of the organization made a comment that struck a chord—"You have such high ethical standards." I thanked her. But I was puzzled. She didn't really know me that well, and we worked in different departments, so where did that comment come from? It wasn't until I started working directly with her that I realized what she meant—I never stopped working, and she saw it based on the emails I was sending at all hours. We were short-staffed at the time, so there was a never-ending supply of work to do. And I had a never-ending supply of desire to prove that I could do all things.

Skip ahead to launching a business as a single mom. I worked hard while getting the company off the ground, and I also worked unusual hours—around the kids' schedules. So when I hired people with boundaries around work and life, I was a little confused about this new breed of people. Who were these people of the "work-life balance" tribe?

Especially in a remote environment, work-life balance can be tricky. It can be easy to get distracted when you need to be on the clock, and it can be hard to shut down and walk away from your computer when you are in the flow. And this is exactly why I became a believer in work-life balance!

To my readers who respond to this term with contempt, you want work-life balance too. Trust me. It's just a really misunderstood term by those who uphold traditional views of work and productivity.

When we describe the typical workday and workweek of the consulting role at WISE, we explain, "To be successful here, protect your time on the clock. When you are on, be 100 percent on without distraction. And protect your time off the clock—be 100 percent off." This is work-life balance.

We have a high-pressure work environment with high expectations, so we need a mentally and emotionally resilient team of highly caring dedicated individuals. The best way to do that is to make sure that people get their downtime. When we notice that a team member is starting to work a schedule that seems to blur the lines by squeezing work and life into small chunks of time throughout the day, we check in. It can be a sign that burnout is not far behind.

Organizational leadership should model work-life balance. I know. I know. I hear you. It's hard for me, too, especially when we are understaffed. Today, I get through the seasons of long hours knowing that balance is just around the corner. And then I snatch it back. I shut my computer down by 4:00 p.m. I go for a walk. I spend time with my family and friends in the evenings. I do things for myself on the weekends.

As a leader, it is important that you are modeling expectations for others. For instance, if you are sending emails at all hours of the night and weekend, your team will feel like that is the expectation and may feel pressured to follow suit.

2. **Create brave spaces.** Brené Brown, author of *Dare to Lead*, provides a lot of great resources to help you determine your values and build a trusting culture. She discusses the importance of creating a brave space that makes it safe to be vulnerable, share insights, be curious, and challenge the status quo. If

this sounds good to you, then I encourage you to check out her books, podcasts, videos, and online resources about this topic.

3. **Practice transparency.** This is a big one. Transparency from the top down is important for creating a safe and trusting environment. It's human nature to want to avoid hard conversations and even justify it by believing you are protecting the agency or the staff. But if there is something big going down with the agency, chances are that your staff can detect your stress from across the building. They hear your hushed tones and see you popping the antacids. And when people don't know the story, they fill in the blanks—creating their own narrative. Transparency feels authentic, and that feels like respect and trust.

4. **Practice active listening.** Initiate listening by checking in with intentionality. Make sure to close the loop in communication to ensure people feel heard. Check out the book *The Way of the Shepherd: Seven Secrets to Managing Productive People*, by Dr. Kevin Leman and Bill Pentak, for valuable insights into the importance of genuine listening and care. And check out *Listen Like You Mean It: Reclaiming the Lost Art of True Connection*, by Ximena Vengoechea, for tips on how to provide a safe space for communication and understanding.

5. **Give feedforward.** As I mentioned, at WISE we have a feedback culture. Our goal is to make expectations clear. Doing so takes the guesswork out of what success looks like. I really like the term *feedforward*, which is a concept developed by business educator and coach Marshall Goldsmith that encourages you to focus on the future as opposed to the past. Feedback tells someone what you *don't* want to see in

actions and behavior, whereas feedforward tells you what you *do* want to see. I love this.

Once I was in a family therapy session with my son. The therapist had him go through an exercise to prepare for the session, which resulted in him sharing a statement: "I am afraid my mom will be disappointed in me." I heard this and launched into a monologue about how he shouldn't worry so much about what I think, which resulted in a very upset kid. I was baffled until the therapist stopped me and said, "I think where this is coming from is that he wants you to be proud of him." Uh, stop the presses! That's all I needed to hear—I was proud of him, so knowing that was what he needed, I could focus on being better at showing that. This example demonstrates the difference between feedback and feedforward. Whereas feedback can cause miscommunication and the receiver to lose sight of the desired behavior, feedforward makes the desired end goal clear. In my example, focusing on the expectation and desired need could have avoided unintentional hurt feelings.

The following suggestions are tactical ways to implement a caring culture:

1. **Anonymous feedback.** Provide opportunities to give anonymous suggestions and feedback, and make sure it is truly anonymous. Once when I was new on a job, I was invited to fill out an anonymous employee survey, which I did with honesty and provided some feedback that I never would have had the guts to share directly with my supervisor. Shortly after, the CEO called our entire department into the conference room and announced that all the negative survey comments

came from our department, and as a result, our supervisor had been terminated. It was a shocking turn of events—and not the only untrustworthy action the CEO ended up taking during my time with the organization—but I vowed then and there to never complete an "anonymous" survey again. Don't be this CEO. Invite feedback, and be willing to hear it and open to recognizing that other people's experiences may be different from your own and equally valid.

2. **Buddy system.** Create a mentoring program for new staff by pairing them with a veteran employee who can answer their questions in a safe space through a regular cadence of communication. It can make being a new employee more comfortable to have a go-to person to ask questions. The mentor can also be a role model for the culture of the organization and help the new employee feel welcome.

3. **Wellness room.** Set aside a room that serves as a physical safe space, and make it culturally acceptable for staff to use the room. Wellness rooms should be quiet, cozy spaces with soft lighting.

4. **Training.** If your programming has your staff working in a high-stress or a secondary-trauma-inducing environment, it is essential that you are conducting appropriate training on secondary trauma, responding to trauma, and other related resources to fully equip your staff. Consider other types of personal development training, like Positive Intelligence,[20] which is designed to help individuals to confront negative self-talk and build mental and emotional resiliency against triggers that can impact coping skills in one's daily life in

---

20   "About | Positive Intelligence," positiveintelligence.com (Positive Intelligence, May 25, 2022), https://www.positiveintelligence.com/about/.

both work and home. At WISE, we have found great benefits in this training and have integrated it into our core professional development program for all staff.

5. **Culture committee.** This committee is made up of employees at all levels of the organization. Members should be paid to participate and have a budget to organize activities for the staff. Consider hosting regular activities like lunches that showcase the different cultures of employees.

6. **Diversity, equity, inclusion, and accessibility (DEIA) committee.** Implement a DEIA committee to evaluate all procedures, policies, and activities through a DEIA lens, and then take action on implementing improvements. We'll cover this in more detail in chapter 8.

7. **Affinity groups.** Affinity groups, also known as employee resource groups (ERGs), are led by employee members and are employer sponsored. Each group is typically a collection of individuals who share a common identity characteristic like gender, sexual orientation, race, nationality, religion, family structure, or physical or mental ability. They create safe spaces for networking, resources for mentorship, and training for professional development. To ensure that affinity groups are adhering to applicable employment and discrimination laws, develop an affinity group policy and training for group leaders.

8. **Flexible paid time off (PTO).** Most organizations have combined sick leave and vacation time into one bucket of time off to be used without having to provide proof of illness, like a doctor's note. This system of time off protects privacy and empowers employees to use their time off for their greatest need.

9. **Mental health days.** It used to be a joke when people would say that they were taking a mental health day. Instead of laughing, normalize mental health days. For work environments that are high stress and have the potential to induce secondary trauma or burnout, consider requiring staff to take a mental health day one time per quarter. Make it clear that mental health is a priority at all levels of the organization. Also consider how the organization will handle seminal events—these are events in which a staff member experiences a traumatic event. It is important that when this occurs, the staff member receives time off and therapeutic support.

10. **Therapy stipend.** Individuals often have barriers to receiving adequate mental health care, including limited or no insurance coverage or lack of access to service providers (many mental healthcare professionals do not take health insurance). Consider providing a therapy stipend or developing a partnership with a community partner that provides therapeutic services on a pro bono or reduced rate for staff. It is also important that an employee assistance program (EAP) is accessible if available. This should be considered when selecting insurance providers. An EAP usually includes a specific number of therapy sessions at no or low cost to employees.

11. **Coaching.** I have found executive coaching to be life changing for me. The right coach relationship can be transformative and serves as an invaluable and empowering resource. At WISE, we provide executive coaching for all staff in supervisory leadership positions. Consider contracting with an executive coach who can work with your leaders one on one and then with teams. They may utilize valuable tools, like the

Enneagram and Positive Intelligence, to help team members become stronger leaders and performers.

12. **Formal performance management system.** Having a formal performance management system is essential to creating a caring environment. Having clear expectations and accountability is liberating. It is far more disconcerting to be told that you are not performing to expectations when you were never provided with clear expectations to begin with. Create a culture in which respectful and direct feedback (or feedforward) is given in real time with clarity, so that there is no confusion and there are no feelings of being blindsided during performance conversations.

Staff Turnover Is Costly

Caring for your staff means giving them the resources and capacity they need to pay that care forward. Making the mistake of expecting them to sacrifice their own well-being in service of your mission is a disservice to your employees *and* your mission. At the least, they will leave. At the worst, they will cause damage on their way out.

> If an organization can't establish a culture of caring for its staff, it faces the likelihood that it will fall into an unsustainable cycle of turnover.

If an organization can't establish a culture of caring for its staff, it faces the likelihood that it will fall into an unsustainable cycle of turnover— hiring and onboarding and hiring and onboarding and hiring and onboarding in seeming perpetuity. That is an expensive loop to be in and raises red flags with key stakeholders like funders and prospective employees.

Hiring costs consist of advertising and interview expenses for all potential candidates, including reference checks, criminal background checks, and other essential prehire queries. Once the candidate has been chosen, onboarding and initial training have their own costs. The new employee is not yet able to fulfill the job for which they've been hired, and the staff member training them is being taken away from their own duties. That downtime costs the organization money.

Rarely does a nonprofit budget for the cost of staff turnover, but even so, it is still paying for it. According to the Work Institute, the cost of employee turnover to an organization is roughly 30 percent (conservatively) of that person's salary.[21] For the median income of a salaried nonprofit worker in the United States ($55,462), this translates to approximately $16,638 per employee departure.

Consider proactively investing that 30 percent into wage increases and other benefits (healthcare, PTO, mental and emotional support systems) to save the organization money in the long term. It will enhance your programs through staffing stability and by virtue of retaining a professional who feels valued and cared for by the organization.

Word to the WISE

Conduct a salary audit and determine ways to support your staff. I know this chapter provides a lot of suggestions. When deciding what changes you want to implement, first ask your team what is most important to them, and prioritize options that may have the greatest immediate impact on your organization's well-being.

---

21   "Work Institute's 2020 Retention Report," https://workinstitute.com/ (Work Institute, 2020), https://info.workinstitute.com/hubfs/2020%20Retention%20Report/ Work%20Institutes%202020%20Retention%20Report.pdf.

CHAPTER

8

PITFALL  8

Your Organization Isn't Serious about Diversity, Equity, Inclusion, and Accessibility

Like many other metropolitan areas, Dallas is a tale of two cities. While the north is home to some of the fastest-growing business sectors in the country, and five of its suburbs are among the wealthiest in the state, southern Dallas embodies a much different story. It is an area facing significant obstacles, and because of Jim Crow laws and redlining—the government-backed practice of denying loans, mortgages, and other services based on a neighborhood's demographics—its residents were cut off from the growth happening elsewhere in the city, causing a systemic lack of resources and entrenched poverty.

WISE has made an intentional commitment to serve the southern sector of Dallas. As a white woman who has benefited from many of the embedded systems designed to disenfranchise my neighbors living in those communities, I believe it is my responsibility—and the duty of the WISE consultancy—to use this position of privilege to do our part to level the playing field.

I am by no means an expert on **diversity, equity, inclusion, and accessibility (DEIA)**. I am an active learner with a deeply held belief that all humans are born with inherent worth and value. My goal in this chapter is to explore this topic in conversation with a mosaic of voices and bring some of that learning to you.

Recognizing Power Dynamics

All power is relational, and the different relationships either reinforce or disrupt one another. The importance of the concept of power to anti-racism is clear: Racism cannot be understood without understanding that power is not only an individual relationship but a cultural one, and that power relationships are shifting constantly.
—RACIAL EQUITY TOOLS

Dr. Froswa' Booker-Drew, PhD, author of *Empowering Charity: A New Narrative of Philanthropy*, is one of the most respected thought leaders in Dallas and beyond. She has an extensive background in nonprofit leadership, partnership development, training, and education. Among many other credits, Froswa' cofounded the South Dallas Employment Project (SDEP), a collective impact organization focused on dismantling the cradle-to-prison pipeline in southern Dallas, and cofounded HERitage Giving Circle, one of the first Black women's

giving circles in Texas. I've had the privilege of working with Froswa'
on the SDEP as well as on her philanthropic and capacity-building
efforts in southern Dallas. I sat down with her to ask about some of
the challenges of implementing DEIA practices.

**Conversations around diversity and equity have called
attention to white privilege. How do you see privilege playing
out in the nonprofit sector?**

Froswa'. As much as we talk about diversity and equity, I don't think
we spend enough time looking at power dynamics that exist within
nonprofit organizations. Those dynamics show up in a variety of
ways, and we can't talk about power dynamics without also looking at
white privilege. For example, if Mr. Jackson and Mrs. Hill are sitting
on a board together, and Mrs. Hill is the vice president of the local
bank, and his loan for his home is at the bank, he's not going to feel
empowered to disagree with her on issues.

That's a power dynamic. Mr. Jackson may nod in agreement
with Mrs. Hill, but that doesn't mean he agrees. It may be that he
feels compelled to comply with the person in power. This is just one
way that power dynamics can impact decision-making of nonprofit
boards in ways that make them less effective. What if Mr. Jackson
wanted to provide input about a recent decision by the bank that
negatively impacted the community and, in doing so, could not only
affect himself personally but alienate his participation in the group?

And this is just one example of the types of dynamics that need
to be considered when building a board to assure there is equity in
that space. The biggest challenge to this is that people don't always
recognize their own privilege and the power that it yields them. But
the fact is we do not all have equal access to the same resources. White

privilege and power must be acknowledged to even begin to create a shift in power dynamics.

How does building diverse boards look different for organizations led by people of color?

Froswa'. There is a very different attitude from organizations led by people of color. Sometimes, there is the perspective that "I am a part of a marginalized population, and our board makeup does reflect those we serve; if I get one or two white people on the board, I'm addressing the issue of diversity." Yet if the organization doesn't address cultural context and competency for those board members, challenges will exist.

The concern for a lot of organizations led by people of color is that "If I bring in too many people that don't look like me, then they won't understand the dynamics that we deal with in our community." There is a fear that bringing in more people who don't understand the community will change the way they do the work. It has happened that more people from outside the community sit on the board, then the mission begins to change, and the way they do business begins to change.

So what I'm often saying to organizations led by people of color, if you bring people in from other communities, you really have to help them understand the work that you do. And I think that goes on both sides. If you sit on the board, you really have to understand the community that you're working in so that cultural context isn't lost.

I have been learning a lot from you about social capital and that it comes in many forms, including information, political power, and connections. It exists in almost every aspect of our lives, and those who have it often don't even realize its

advantage or influence. How does social capital impact non-profits led by people of color?

Froswa'. I don't think white-led nonprofits appreciate their own social capital and how it enables those organizations to raise more money. They have the networks that connect them to larger funders. Nonprofits led by people of color don't have the same access to funding networks. [22] They tend to be more grassroots. You are more likely to see those nonprofits doing significant work in the community on shoestring budgets and unpaid or underpaid staff working tirelessly to improve the conditions of the communities they love. To help remedy this, funders need to do a better job of purposely helping nonprofits led by people of color with both general operating and capacity building funds as well as making introductions to their boards and donors to build their network.

More and more funders are requiring their grant applicants to provide a statement about the agency's DEIA efforts. During the rise of the Black Lives Matter movement, we began to require that all of our clients have a DEIA statement. What we found is that some clients had already been intentional about DEIA efforts, some were trying to move forward in a thoughtful way in this space, and others weren't getting it or were even actively resisting it. How do you encourage people to develop and implement DEIA in their organizations?

---

22 "58 percent of BIPOC-led (Black, Indigenous, People of Color) organizations received corporate donations in 2021, compared with 71 percent of white-led groups. Twenty-six percent of BIPOC-led nonprofits received at least half of their fiscal 2021 support as unrestricted funding, compared with 41 percent of white-led nonprofits." Dan Parks, "Deep Disparities Persist in Finances of Nonprofits Led by White People and People of Color," philanthropy.com (*The Chronicle of Philanthropy*, June 8, 2022), https://www.philanthropy.com/article/deep-disparities-persist-in-finances-of-nonprofits-led-by-white-people-and-people-of-color.

Froswa'. One of the things I've been really apprehensive about is pushing DEIA training. I don't think organizations should start off with training until they understand the problems they are trying to solve. If you don't know why your organization has a DEIA problem, then training only serves as a ritual of feeling good. I always suggest that an organization perform a diversity audit first. It opens an organization's eyes to their blind spots, then they can participate in DEIA training to fix what they now realize is broken. I recommend reviewing some of the resources available from Racial Equity Tools, as well as using entities like Dallas Truth and Racial Healing as a resource in identifying potential consultants that can assist in this work.

The Roundtable

To understand others' experiences with DEIA issues, I brought together a diverse roundtable of nonprofit professionals to share observations and insights. All have spent a minimum of five years working in nonprofits. To protect identities, names have been changed (other than mine). Some of the conversation has been annotated for ease of reading.

> **Tawnia.** It seems like the country has suddenly woken up to the entrenched racism that has always been here and is starting to take a stand against it. Funders are starting to demand that nonprofits explain their efforts with DEIA. Talk about your experiences working in the nonprofit sector as they relate to DEIA.

> **Lily.** I think one of the basic hurdles with DEIA work is that so many nonprofits don't track the demographics of the people they serve, their staff, or their boards. It's not even on

their radar to do so, or they just don't want to put the effort into doing it. But if you aren't tracking this information, how could you possibly ensure that the leadership and staff are reflective of the people you serve?

Tawnia. I'm glad that funders are pushing nonprofits in this way because so many resist this work and don't even see its value. And even nonprofits with good intentions of diversifying their boards, leadership teams, and employees get distracted by other priorities. So if their funding is tied to it, maybe they will be forced to take action.

Lily. I agree, but I also think some organizations will just try to do the bare minimum to check the box.

Tawnia. I'm not sure that nonprofits will be able to get away with that for long. We had a client who recently lost significant grant funding, and the funder explained that it really came down to their DEIA efforts. It's an organization with an all-white staff and an almost completely white board. It primarily serves Black and Hispanic kids. Their position on DEIA was something akin to: "Our board chair [the wealthy white husband of the founder] hires Black people at his company." The founder tried to argue with the funder, but I think the funder's response was basically, "We see you, and we don't like what we see."

Barb. It's important for nonprofits to do a better job of closing the gap between the leadership's perspective and intentions and the needs of the community they are trying to serve. It is common to hear "We're offering help to the underserved; why aren't *they* taking advantage of it? They clearly don't want to help themselves." My first question when I hear this is, "How have you engaged the people you think need your help in developing the solution?" It's amazing how many nonprofit leaders have never thought from this perspective. They simply identify what *they* think is a problem and then they create what *they* think is the solution.

Hannah. I know exactly what you mean! I worked for an organization that received a lot of funding to establish a summer youth program. Just prior to launch, the program director presented the program to the fundraising team. He shared all the great activities it would provide to keep kids off the streets over the summer. I asked, "How are the kids going to get to the community center in order to participate in the program?" He said, "Well, their parents are going to drive them." I explained, "But the program is six miles away from the neighborhood you are hoping to serve; many parents do not have cars, or they work long hours. They don't have the luxury of dropping off and picking up their children from camp six miles from their house." The director was angry with me, but he had no frame of reference for the community he was trying to serve and was unable to anticipate their needs.

Lily. And then they wonder why they can't establish trust in the communities they are serving. One of the key tenets of DEIA work is including more voices and perspectives to develop responsive programs and services.

Candace. That leads back to the point about the DEIA checkbox. I have served in leadership roles at several organizations, and I'm typically the only person of color. One issue I've seen at many organizations is that diversity efforts quickly turn into tokenism. There is this undertone that you're meant to be seen and not heard, and if you do show up authentically, you are not well received. This is especially evident around difficult conversations; you're meant to blend into the conversation

> **One issue I've seen at many organizations is that diversity efforts quickly turn into tokenism. There is this undertone that you're meant to be seen and not heard, and if you do show up authentically, you are not well received.**

without bringing up very real issues that require people to have to sit in discomfort.

Barb. Or you are expected to represent the voice of all Black people or all people of color in general, which is a ridiculous expectation. It's like that show *Insecure* and the nonprofit Issa worked at, We Got Y'all! I love that the show called attention to **white saviorism**.

Candace. Remember when they revealed the new logo, and it was a white hand holding up Black kids? So cringy!

Robin. One of the most outright shocking examples of white saviorism I've seen was with an annual appeal letter. On one side, a white mother was depicted reading a book to her child. It said, "Johnny lives in zip code *X*. His parents read to him every night and make sure he has enough food to eat and his medical needs are met." The other side had a picture of a Hispanic boy alone, looking sad. It said, "Carlos, in zip code *X*, has a single mom who works two jobs. She doesn't speak English and doesn't have time to read to him. He often goes hungry, and his vaccinations aren't up to date." I think the founder of this organization, an older white man, really had no idea how racist this appeal was and how it also blamed the recipients of their services for their circumstances—painting the mother as less capable or caring. I tried to point this out to him, and he just dismissed my concerns.

Tawnia. Can you imagine how a family being served by that agency would feel if they got ahold of that letter? That kind of narrative reflects the fact that the founder sees them as "the other" and flawed.

Hannah. That reminds me of a similar story about an appeal piece that tried to inappropriately change the appearance of the family being highlighted on the cover. This was actually at a previous consulting firm that I worked at. I was responsible for interviewing the family to highlight in the success story. It was a terrific story about how a husband and wife with small children went from being homeless to having new jobs and all of their kids were in school and happy. The picture for the front of the appeal was the family beaming with pride and happiness. When we got the piece back to review it before sharing it with the client, the design team had photoshopped out their tattoos! I refused to send it to the client that way and fought to have the photo changed back. What is even the point of that? To deny someone's authentic self to make the reader feel more comfortable?

Candace. Wow! That is terrible. Can you imagine how that family would have felt if they saw that picture? I am so proud of you for standing your ground. It's almost like a denial of another person's humanity to pander to people who live in a bubble of privilege.

Hannah. I learned a valuable lesson early in my nonprofit career about not being afraid to confront privileged donors. As we know, in nonprofit, people with the money are king, and sometimes they abuse that power. When I worked for a performing arts organization, one of the agency's biggest donors would hang out with the staff during intermission. He would often drink and then start saying inappropriate things. At one event, he asked me where I was from, and when I told him, he went on a rant about how there are too many Jewish people in that neighborhood. Our executive director overheard him and immediately shut it down. He told the donor it was inappropriate and that he is not allowed to speak to any of the staff like that, and that we didn't need his money if this was how he was going to behave. This is a donor who gave six-figure gifts to the organization and had underwritten a capital campaign. That was a defining moment for me personally. Just because somebody has a lot of money doesn't mean they can do or say whatever they want. I think that can be a challenge for some nonprofits—it is certainly not the path of least resistance when you are trying to raise funds. Even when you know it is the right thing to do, it takes a lot of courage to draw that line.

Robin. In the DEIA conversation, accessibility is a topic often overlooked. I have attended several fundraisers in which the organizers were so focused on the flash and awe of the venue that they never considered its lack of accessibility. There is actually a children's theater in the city that doesn't have a wheelchair ramp in the auditorium. I want to see more conversation around accessibility of services for people with physical, developmental, and intellectual differences.

Finding the Path Forward

It is not uncommon for a fundraising assessment conducted by WISE to reveal challenges related to HR. In these cases, we refer our clients to Gabriela Norton, the founder, president and CEO of People Performance Resources (PPR), LLC, a human resources consulting firm based in Dallas.

In writing this chapter, I turned to Gabriela to gain insights on how her firm works with clients to implement DEIA policies and procedures.

How do you go about helping an organization implement a DEIA strategy?

Gabriela. It goes beyond just checking a box. DEIA must become part of the fabric of the organization, and it should be tailored to that organization's purpose.

For a client we recently supported in the creation of their DEIA program, our first suggestion was the launch of a committee that represented every area of their business to lead these efforts that will rotate annually to allow new team members to participate. They invited all teams to volunteer, culminating in a seven-person committee that met one hour per week for twelve weeks. The committee first learned about **unconscious bias**, then spent the next week observing it in their lives and work environments, and then came back to the committee to report their learnings. This exercise was incredibly helpful and really eye-opening for them. It led the way to the next activity, a *SWOT (Strengths, Weaknesses, Opportunities and Threats) analysis* to talk through the organization's SWOT from a DEIA perspective.

The committee then came up with a plan of action to create systemic change within the organization. They first developed a DEIA statement that, at completion, was showcased in the employee handbook and on their website. They then began to engage further into the organization and their specific teams, gathering feedback through a DEIA lens and bringing it back to the committee. They came up with ten action items that they narrowed down to three to focus on first. They developed a process to tackle each of these areas for improvement.

As a result of these efforts, the process of hiring took on a totally different approach. They thought about how they wanted to demonstrate a diverse and welcoming organization to candidates who are interviewing and came up with ideas on how to invite more team members into those conversations. They revamped the performance management system. For transparency and accountability, they also implemented an annual survey to determine how they will continue to improve year over year.

Can you talk about how this committee was supported by the organization's leadership?

Gabriela. It is important that the DEIA statement has feedback from a good variety of constituencies. In this case, they invited feedback at the board level and from their communications team. The committee even asked the board to get feedback from their networks. This is an example of practicing inclusivity of perspectives. Getting as many perspectives as possible while vetting the statement is important because the ultimate DEIA statement holds the organization accountable at all levels.

We had a client recently with a board that wouldn't even discuss DEIA. Anytime the topic was brought up, they would dismiss it. How do you think this kind of refusal will impact organizations?

Gabriela. When leadership lacks self-awareness around their internal biases, it can be very damaging. I had a client who hired a Latina CEO. The board was all white and mostly family members. It was painful to watch them continually dismiss her. Someone literally told her that she was "too ethnic." Part of the reason that I am so inspired to do this work is because I know what it feels like to be dismissed for not being fluent in English. Early in my career, I was not given a professional opportunity because I mispronounced two words in my interview. I was told my accent made those words sound like something else. I was devastated, especially since I knew I was well qualified for the role.

I had another client that asked their top job candidate to not talk about their sexual identity if they were to be hired. While some organizations feel strongly on social issues based on their religious beliefs, if you want to be competitive and retain talent, you have to be more accepting of someone's identity. This work takes so much intentional effort and investment of resources. You have to make it a priority and take it seriously. When an organization refuses to do the work needed to dismantle their own biases, they will likely struggle to survive.

I have found that younger generations seem to have an inherent belief that all people deserve respect and practice much more

acceptance and curiosity about people's differences. What are
your thoughts about this generational difference?

Gabriela. You are spot-on about this younger generation demanding more acceptance for themselves and those around them. Those who refuse to practice inclusivity and acceptance will be left behind. These younger generations are really watching and paying attention to whether you walk the talk. You are either participating in becoming a more inclusive nation, or you are not. Younger employees will not stick around if they feel like the employer is not authentic in their inclusivity, and those organizations will not continue to be competitive.

We all have an opportunity to demonstrate what positive impact looks like in DEIA and to own when we fall short. I always like to encourage people to give themselves and each other grace throughout the process, and I like to quote Dr. Maya Angelou, who said, "Do the best that you can until you know better, and then when you know better, do better."

A Funder's Perspective

My final interview is with a local funder who has made a priority of reviewing applications and the work of nonprofits through a DEIA lens. I wanted to get a sense of what they were looking for during their grant-application review process and how they see DEIA continuing to impact decisions by the funding community.

You are one of the funders who has taken a hard stance on using a DEIA lens to review and score grant applications. I am eager to hear more about how you developed the framework and rubric you used.

Funder. We used the Trust-Based Philanthropy Project framework. Our goal is to use our resources to eliminate racial disparities and focus on building an anti-racist organization and community.

To prepare for this funding cycle, we had a committee of ten staff members who spent a lot of time developing the three questions used in the application to assess how applicants were addressing diversity and inclusivity in their work. Our questions were intended to get an understanding of how they were involving clients in their work, how the demographics of employees and volunteers reflect the population they are serving, and what their plans are for increasing diversity and racial equity education within the organization.

In the previous application, our question about efforts in diversity and equity resulted in many organizations submitting their antidiscrimination policy. That wasn't helpful. There is a big difference between having an antidiscrimination policy and making intentional efforts at being a diverse and inclusive organization.

WISE RESOURCES

The Trust-Based Philanthropy Project is a peer-to-peer learning and advocacy initiative to make trust-based practices the norm in philanthropy. Recognizing the inherent power imbalance between foundations and nonprofits, philanthropy will be more successful, rewarding, and effective if funders approach their grantee relationships from a place of trust, humility, and transparency.

> We had a client who was previously funded by you and didn't move past the first round of review during this cycle. The feedback they received was that they weren't doing enough

around diversity and inclusion. They were very defensive and dismissive of the validity of that feedback. I'm curious about how you evaluated applicants' responses to the three questions.

Funder. We knew going into the review process that a lot of organizations were not doing this work yet. When that was the case, we wanted to see a plan of action for how they would move more intentionally into this work. For instance, on a basic level, we want to see that nonprofits are tracking the demographics of staff and board members. They would receive additional points for involving the community they serve in the organization, for staff and volunteers reflecting the people they serve, and for their plan for the implementation of DEIA efforts. Having a board and staff that reflects, and better yet, includes people they serve is important. People respond better to those from, or representative of, their community.

What are some other ways you changed your grant-making process to be more accessible to organizations led by people of color?

Funder. Over the past several years, we have been intentional in building relationships with organizations led by and serving people of color—focusing on those areas of the city that have been historically segregated and oppressed. One of our goals in building these relationships was to give them access to us so that they could ask questions and advocate for themselves in ways they have not historically been able to. This is about building social capital.

During the last grant cycle, we had a goal of trying to fund more diverse organizations that hadn't been funded in the past. So if there was an organization doing diversity and inclusivity well, it would boost their score. We also zeroed in on target geography by looking at zip code data with preference for organizations that are in their community, serving their community. We also removed some of the audit requirements for smaller organizations to be more inclusive of those from disenfranchised communities that were historically not eligible to apply. We were excited to see many organizations apply for the first time ever. Throughout the entire process, we tried to keep the same ratio of diverse applicants consistent across decision points.

I have no doubt the responses to your diversity and inclusion questions were revealing. We used to have a client, a large and well-known service provider, who would decline funding that would require them to sign an antidiscrimination statement because it was in conflict with their religious doctrine. This is one of the reasons they are no longer a client. I'm curious how you see this new trend of funders focused on social justice impacting faith-based organizations that have discriminatory practices.

Funder. This will likely be a focus in the next application development process—getting at the heart of whether an organization provides services without discriminating against a specific group of people.

I think some nonprofits see this current focus on racial equity and justice as a trend that may lose steam. What do you see as the future of this focus with funders?

Funder. It's true that social justice / racial equity funds are trendy. If a funder is serious about this work, it will permeate through all the organization's processes. Our hope is to see more funders take steps to make their overall grant-making process more equitable. Carving out a million dollars from a funder's overall funding to create a racial equity fund isn't really creating racial equity. Institutionalizing processes that make the entire grant-making process more accessible, equitable, and focused on funding organizations that make this work a priority—that is what will really move the needle.

Unconscious Bias

As a society, we have entrenched beliefs, narratives, and systems that impact how we experience the world. One memorable example I have about this is when my young daughter was explaining all of the expensive things she would buy when she grew up—like a Tesla and a mansion. "You had better marry a rich man," I actually started to say. I couldn't believe myself. I was startled that I'd say something so absurd to her.

I was single when I adopted my kids, and shortly after, I began building a company and everything we have from ground zero. Yet there I was, about to tell my daughter she would need to marry a man to get what she wanted? It was almost automatic as a result of the kind of rhetoric I heard growing up.

How many biased narratives like this one do we harbor in quiet corners of our minds? This matters greatly when we work in service with and for other people. In the world of nonprofits, our narratives—mental, verbal, written—along with our actions, reveal how we see others.

Asset-based language is a framework that pushes us to think about the individuals we serve as capable people who can be empowered with tools and education.

For instance, review the language you use to talk about the people you serve. Are you talking about them in a way that would make them feel comfortable if they heard or read the narrative? Often, we use outdated terminology or phrases to describe people and their needs without really thinking about it.

Asset-based language is a framework that pushes us to think about the individuals we serve as capable people who can be empowered with tools and education. It shifts our perspective to see that systems, not people, are what is broken, and to emphasize people's strengths, not deficits. Words such as "vulnerable" and "at-risk" position individuals as having a deficit, reinforcing stereotypes that some individuals have inherent character flaws or defects. Even referring to the population you serve with the term "these," as in "these moms," indicates a perception that "they are different from me." And overused phrases like "We provide a hand up, not a handout" are condescending and imply a need for the program participants to prove worthiness.

Instead, focus on how circumstances have impacted the ability of some individuals to leverage their inherent strengths and assets. Using this asset-based language filter, read through your marketing, communications, and fundraising materials.

Take this a step further, and consider how you involve and empower the individuals you serve. Ask yourself these questions as a starting point:

- Are clients involved in the program design?

- Are there feedback loops so clients can impact program changes?

- Are you trusting clients to determine their own needs and empowering them to seek their own solutions?

- Are you walking alongside clients in solidarity or trying to save them from the problems *you've* determined they have with the solutions *you've* determined they need?

- Do you hire staff and recruit board members from the population you serve?

- Do your board members or organizational leadership have lived experience in your mission work?

GETTING IT WISE: OF THE COMMUNITY, SERVING THE COMMUNITY

During fiscal year 2021, Baker Street clients served were 65 percent Black, 32 percent Hispanic, and 51 percent female. Baker Street's board of directors is 60 percent female, 50 percent white/non-Hispanic, 40 percent Black, and 10 percent Hispanic or Latinx. Baker Street currently has thirteen staff members. Nine are female, and four are male; twelve are Black, and one is white/non-Hispanic.

Baker Street is broadly guided by a deep intention to provide equitable programs that respond to the needs of the community. Taking on the systemic oppression of a historically Black community, Baker Street is a Black-founded and Black-led organization. The leadership team and the majority of staff are from the community and have personal experience with the issues Baker Street seeks to solve. A leadership team that mirrors the community is imperative in exposing oppression, creating systems of equity and advancing justice.

As a place-based nonprofit, Baker Street works with community members to identify and address the systemic effects of institutional racism. A leadership council of community members guides Baker Street strategy and informs the organization's work. The Baker Street board continually seeks additional board members from the community.

The Baker Street Liberators Fellowship, the organization's flagship advocacy program, influences systemic change supported by Baker

Street. Fellows are adults who live or work in the community and are selected through an application and interview process. They are equipped with the knowledge, connections and skills to create ways to benefit the community by focusing on equity-based programs. The Fellows voice their personal experiences when facing challenges in the community and create systems of equity and programs to reimagine the education system.

There has been movement away from using "client" to identify the individuals being served. Many organizations use "neighbor" or "apprentice" for workforce programs. I love this idea and use "client" in this book, as it is still the most common term used to refer to the constituents served by nonprofits.

WISE RESOURCES

DEIA self-audits are not a one-size-fits-all process. Several organizations have developed helpful resources for nonprofits to get started on this work, including Racial Equity Tools, Coalition of Communities of Color (CCC), ADA National Network, and the Annie E. Casey Foundation.

Additional resources:

- Racial Equity Tools (racialequitytools.org)

- Coalition of Communities of Color (coalitioncommunitiescolor.org)

- Operationalizing Equity - The Annie E. Casey Foundation (aecf.org)

- H2H-Language-Guide_A-Resource-for-Using-Asset-Based-Language-with-Young-People.pdf (heretohere.org)

- ABSTRACT (cpb-us-w2.wpmucdn.com)

- Trust-Based Philanthropy (trustbasedphilanthropy.org)

Word to the WISE

Conduct a DEIA self-audit. It takes a level of humility to step back and take an honest look at your organization. For nonprofits, it can be even more challenging to acknowledge these deficits because most of us come to this work with good intentions and a desire to share our time, talents, and money to help others—how could anything be wrong with that? But even the best of intentions can be misguided or have unintended consequences. If we truly want to do good work and build a strong, sustainable organization, we must be willing to see beyond our own perspectives by creating a safe and equitable environment that includes many voices in the decision-making process.

PITFALL **9**

Your Fundraising Goals Are Unreasonable

You've figured out your financials, identified funding streams, shown your volunteers some love, engaged your community, strengthened your board, mapped out a care plan for your staff, and diversified the voices in your organization. Now it's time to create a development plan that will bring it all to the next level.

I always recommend that a development plan, which serves as an organization's annual fundraising strategy, be created either before or during the budgeting process. If this is done afterward, you could be committing your organization to revenue goals that are unreachable. Remember, funders will be evaluating your fiscal management based, in part, on performance toward your budget. So set yourself up for success.

Unfortunately, there is no turnkey development plan. Each plan must be uniquely developed based on the organization's readiness, assets, and needs. The biggest mistake is to make it unrealistic. The second biggest mistake is to not make it measurable and detailed enough to serve its purpose—as a frequently updated document that helps track progress toward your goals.

Evaluating Organizational Readiness, Assets, and Resources

At WISE, when working with clients to create a development plan, we always begin with a fundraising assessment. This is our thorough review of an organization's fundraising operations and history, and it involves several important considerations.

ARE YOU A GOOD INVESTMENT?

Every investor wants to know their money won't be wasted. Know the answers to these important questions to help your fundraising strategy succeed:

What Are Your Cash Reserves?

As mentioned in chapter 3, organizations should have a minimum of six months of cash reserves in the bank. If you don't have the minimum level, your development plan needs to include a strategy to build those reserves.

How Much Are You Investing in Your Programs?

Your 990 Part IX should reflect that you're spending at least 75 percent of your expenses on programs. As described in chapter 3, if financial documents show that you don't have an appropriate level of investment in programs, prioritize rightsizing expense ratios. In the meantime, your development plan needs to consider the impact of this on your grant-writing strategy. You will also need to have a strategy for how to communicate about your expense ratios. We use the sustainability statement section of a grant proposal to do this.

How Involved Is Your Board in Fundraising?

In chapter 6, we discussed the importance of the board as a multiplier of capacity and connections. If your board is not involved in fundraising (as a connector and donor), then your development plan should include a strategy to engage it.

How Stable Is Your Funding?

Funders want to have confidence that your organization will exist six months from now. If your funding mix is not diverse and you are overly reliant on a single source or type of revenue, you need to include a strategy to increase individual giving.

DO YOU HAVE ACCOUNTABILITY TOOLS IN PLACE?

The development plan, with **SMART (specific, measurable, achievable, realistic, and timebound)** goals, is the cornerstone of accountability. This means every person who participates in fundraising has formal, individual, measurable goals associated with the overall fundraising goal, and each fundraising activity has a defined strategy. Answer these questions to see if you are set up to achieve your fundraising goals:

Do You Have a Goal-Based Performance Management System?

In chapter 1, we covered the importance of having a formal performance management system from a risk-mitigation perspective, one based on goals that makes expectations clear and ensures everyone is on the same page. Organizational performance goals for fundraising staff should mirror the development plan.

Do You Have a Dynamic Donor Database?

"Dynamic" means that you can analyze data in a more flexible and complex way than a donor list kept in other formats like a spreadsheet or financial system. A dynamic donor database is designed to give you the ability to run reports so your decisions can be data driven. Some helpful data points include year-to-date progress by donor type or strategy, lapsed donors, donor retention, and year-to-date comparisons.

Of course, your reports will only be useful if the data is accurate and current, as well as specific when it comes to coding gifts toward source and initiative. More sophisticated platforms or integrated solutions can provide additional information like connectivity to other people, companies or groups, and **prospect scoring** based on giving history and public data.

At the highest level of functionality, the database is used to track prospect pipelines. When you are assessing progress toward your fundraising goals, looking at the total committed or received is only part of the picture. You also want to assess the *probability* that you will achieve your goal.

Let's say you have three months left in the fiscal year and a $200,000 gap in grant revenue. To determine whether you can close that gap on time, look at what grant requests are currently pending and the projected timing of those decisions. If the value of those asks doesn't even add up to $200,000, your goal is out of reach. Knowing this now gives you an opportunity to add more prospects to the pipeline or to implement a **gap strategy**.

WISE PRO TIP: TRACK PROBABILITY TO VALUE YOUR DONOR PIPELINE

If you are like me, you won't just want to have enough asks out to reach the goal, but you'll also want to use a rating system to track the probability of receiving a gift. You could assign a 25 percent probability to a cold ask of a donor with no connection to the organization, 50 percent to a warm lead with no current giving, 75 to an ask that is based in relationship or giving history, and 90 percent to an ask you feel is almost a done deal, like a verbal commitment before a signed agreement. So if you made a cold ask of $100,000, your probability rating would be 25 percent. Multiplying those figures results in the value of that ask—$25,000. Assigning probabilities gives you a sense of the current value of your pipeline and the likelihood you will hit your goal.

Your rating system should make sense for your organization. I would lower or increase the rating percentages depending on your track record with community impact, credibility and standing in the community, and historical rate of return for the strategy. It's best to judge these conservatively.

WHAT ARE YOUR ASSETS?

When creating your development plan, leverage your assets. Doing this will give you greater efficiency in your fundraising strategies. To determine your assets, schedule a brainstorming session. In addition to fundraising staff and volunteers, you may want to consider inviting other stakeholders, such as an involved donor, to participate. During this session, use the questions below to make three lists.

1. What Do You Do Really Well?

Brainstorm with your team to determine what your organization does very well. In addition to fundraising activities, think about programmatic activities, access to populations, and media reach. Leave nothing off the table. Thinking outside the box can generate some of the most innovative fundraising strategies.

2. What Are Your Staff and Volunteer Strengths?

For the purpose of this conversation, your team is composed of the people who support your fundraising initiatives. What talents do you have on your team? Is everyone maximizing their potential? What professional development opportunities or interests do team members have that could bring new skills to the team?

3. What Resources Could You Leverage?

List every resource you can think of, including staff, volunteers, donors, marketing opportunities, and community partners. Is there a special donor relationship that is of particular benefit? Explore how each resource impacts the organization. Think positively here. In nonprofits, it's easy to look at resources from the perspective of needing more. What factors make your resources assets beyond face value?

Once you've listed all assets, narrow the list down. Combine any duplicated or similar assets. Check to ensure that everyone understands why an asset is considered to be one.

To further narrow your list, follow these steps:

First, create a ranking system (1 = minimal revenue opportunity, 2 = some revenue opportunity, and 3 = good revenue opportunity) and rank each asset. Now focus only on those that have the highest level of revenue opportunity.

As you think through this, consider these questions:

- Is there an asset you can sell (a programmatic workshop, naming or logo opportunities for physical spaces or wearables, access to an audience through a conference, etc.)?

- Is there an asset that would provide access to new resources (introductions by influential major donors to other donors, highly invested corporate partner to their vendors, business owners to their peers, etc.)?

- Does someone have a skill or talent that is not being leveraged (social media, design, marketing, technical writing skills, etc.)?

Second, rank your assets according to how strongly they are associated with existing fundraising strategies or activities (1 = no association with an existing strategy, 2 = some association, and 3 = a clear association). Focus primarily on assets that rank the highest.

While making this list, ask whether you are currently maximizing each asset. You may have listed an asset because it is already being leveraged in an impactful way—consider ways that you can leverage the asset across multiple fundraising activities. For instance, are you packaging multiple sponsorship opportunities? Are you cross-promoting sponsorships at the events, such as including a golf sponsorship in your gala's silent auction? Is there a way that you can better leverage a strength to improve a current initiative?

By now, you should have a list of assets that have a high level of revenue potential for use in an existing strategy. One last question: Can you leverage them within your current capacity this year? Prioritize these assets as you build your development plan.

Understanding Donors and Giving Methods

Before diving into the nuts and bolts of creating the development plan itself, let's review the three major private revenue sources (government grants were covered in detail in chapter 3), along with their most common motivations and giving vehicles. While this information may be geared more toward small nonprofits with limited capacity, nonprofits of any size can be helped by the fundraising best practices outlined here.

Don't try to fit all these strategies into your development plan. Remember that your situation is unique. Your organization and your fundraising team have their own strengths, assets, and capacity limitations. Use these best practices to maximize and protect your capacity and develop a reasonable development plan.

INDIVIDUAL DONORS

> **For the purposes of creating your development plan, you need to make a robust individual-giving plan a top priority. Capacity must be carved out for this.**

As mentioned, individual giving is the most sustainable type of giving. If it dominates your revenue streams, celebrate it—as long as it isn't coming from only a few donors. Be concerned, however, if it makes up only a small percentage of your revenue (less than one-third). For the purposes of creating your development plan, you need to make a robust individual-giving plan a top priority. Capacity must be carved out for this.

Motivations

While there are probably just as many complex reasons why people give as there are people who give, here are some common motivations:

- A personal connection to the mission that compels them to fulfill their need to cause change, ease a burden, or return a generosity bestowed upon them

- An invitation to get involved or give by someone they care about

- A desire to make an impact on an issue, community need, or current crisis

- An opportunity to deepen their commitment and increase their personal impact (if they are already volunteers or participants)

- A need to receive recognition within or gain access to a social group

- A desire to leave a legacy by giving a gift that is significant enough to outlive them (i.e., naming opportunities or other public recognition of a major gift, establishing an endowment or scholarship fund)

- A chance to be part of a major undertaking, like a capital or innovative project, that gives them access to insider knowledge and an opportunity to feel connected to something exciting happening in the community

- A need to gain access to an experience (i.e., mission trips, voluntourism)

- A desire to show respect and appreciation for someone (i.e., honor and memorial giving)

Donors may be steered by one or more of these motivations or by others not listed. Either way, understand these different forces so you can provide opportunities for people to meet their needs by giving to your mission.

Giving Strategies

These are the most common methods of individual giving and the strategies we typically recommend to our clients when helping them create their development plan.

MAJOR GIFTS

A major gift is defined as the minimum donation amount from a single source that is considered significant to the organization. It is likely a dollar amount that would trigger an elevated outreach of appreciation, like a phone call from the executive director. It can be $250 or $50,000. This amount is different for every organization. Note that I am referring to major gifts for individual donors. A major gift may be defined differently for *institutional donors*.

> All donors are valuable to an organization, so why is it so important to distinguish a major gift? Because it's best to use more of your limited capacity to cultivate donors who are currently giving at this level, or have the potential to, in a more intentional way.

One way you can determine the minimum major individual gift for your organization is to analyze your donations from individuals over the past couple of years. Remove any anomalies (large gifts that far exceed your next highest amount), and then segment your donors by range of gift size. There should be a distinct dollar amount in which roughly the top 5 percent (based on number of donors and not total giving) of your donors fall into.

If you have, say, 345 donors and the top 14 donors (14/345 = 6 percent) are giving $2,500, this would be a good minimum individual major gift for your nonprofit.

All donors are valuable to an organization, so why is it so important to distinguish a major gift? Because it's best to use more of your limited capacity to cultivate donors who are currently giving at this level, or have the potential to, in a more intentional way. Consider this: when your pipes freeze and burst, and your organization needs $20,000 for immediate repairs, are you going to write a grant application for that or implement a fundraising event? No. The need for fast money requires relationships with people who can give at a level that is significant to your nonprofit and can make quick decisions.

Carry this forward into the context of your annual development plan. Which strategy maximizes your capacity? Building a relationship with a committed donor who gives $10,000 per year and will support your mission through thick and thin or implementing a golf tournament that nets $10,000? In your plan, set a goal for the number of individual donors and amount of major gift revenue you want to have this fiscal year.

ANNUAL CAMPAIGNS

A successful annual campaign will bring in sustainable, unrestricted revenue and build long-term donor relationships. While people often use these terms interchangeably, an annual appeal is different from an annual campaign. Annual appeals are specific asks and may be included in an annual

> A successful annual campaign will bring in sustainable, unrestricted revenue and build long-term donor relationships.

campaign. The most common annual appeal is the year-end appeal letter.

A single stand-alone appeal is limited in its ability to reach donors and bring in revenue. It is a very passive strategy. Instead, we recommend integrating appeals into a high-touch annual campaign. These are eight best practices that we utilize for campaigns:

1. **Set a goal.** Set a realistic stretch goal for your annual campaign. To come up with this, analyze previous campaign giving, special giving appeals, and overall individual giving. While we recommend that you keep your campaign goal focused on unrestricted revenue, it is helpful to create a theme with language that explains the importance of the goal. What can the revenue do for your organization? Create a gift chart that shows the different levels of giving and how they can help serve your mission.

2. **Determine your time frame.** We recommend a three-month campaign. If you stretch your annual campaign longer, it will linger on, lose momentum, and become unfocused. Giving your campaign a deadline will ensure that you have revenue when you need it and keep the momentum going until the goal is met.

3. **Integrate other individual-giving activities.** Are you conducting a giving-day campaign? Do you have a giving society? Are you soliciting event sponsorship? Are you hosting an open house? Consider how you can integrate your activities into your campaign plan so that you don't confuse donors or burn them out with too many uncoordinated asks. You may need to combine asks or cancel activities that conflict with your campaign plan.

4. **Segment donors.** As you develop your plan, run a report of donors who have given during the last three to five years. Review their total annual giving and their largest single gift for each year, and note whether this gift was tied to a specific giving opportunity. Now segment your donors into at least three categories: those who can give major gifts, those who can give significant gifts, and those who will likely give small gifts. Consider utilizing a prospect-screening tool to help you determine segmentation. This process is a combination of analyzing data and using your knowledge about your donors. Based on which segment they're in, you will engage them in different ways during the campaign.

5. **Recruit a committee.** Recruit a campaign chair and a committee of volunteers who are dedicated to helping you reach your goal. Give them clear job descriptions that define both their roles and your expectations. Train them on the campaign plan. Ask them to help you sign letters, thank donors, reach out to previous donors, and invite new prospects to learn more about the organization. We like to ask campaign committee members to do something like "Take five, bring five," in which they take five existing donors to cultivate and then introduce five prospective donors to the organization. They will focus on major donors through peer outreach. It is important that you are intentional in how you prepare and support your committee members by providing training, timelines, templates, scripts, and tour and volunteer opportunities to attend with donors.

6. **Take advantage of a silent phase for leadership giving.** Review the list of donors in your top segment. They are most

likely to give major gifts and are the ones you should engage at the beginning of your campaign. Schedule a time to meet with them in person to tell them about your campaign. Thank them for being a mission partner, and ask if they would consider serving on the committee and giving a leadership gift. Be specific with your requests, and explain how their participation in the campaign will motivate others to do the same. You need their help to be successful. One or more of these donors may be a challenge gift prospect; give them an option to let you leverage their gift for a greater impact by inviting other donors to match it during the public phase of the campaign.

7. **Be high touch.** Your campaign should include thank-you calls to previous donors, invitations to meetings, and tours and volunteer opportunities. This is how you create engaged long-term donors. Your committee will help you with these efforts.

8. **Steward your donors.** After the campaign is over, have a plan for how you will steward donors throughout the year.

SUSTAINED GIVING

The two primary sustained giving strategies we recommend for individuals are monthly giving and giving societies. These types of strategies are ideal because the gifts are recurring. A giving society is a membership-based group that supports the mission of an organization. It typically requires a minimum donation, provides benefits to members, and is peer led. It can be challenging to implement, and it is common for nonprofits to have a false launch, but these tips will help develop a successful one.

1. **Define a major gift.** Use the method previously described earlier to define a major gift. This will be the minimum donation amount to join the giving society. You could even create multiple giving societies based on common interests of your donors (e.g., young professionals, women, men).

2. **Establish a fundraising goal.**

    - Step 1: Count the number of major donors you currently have. If you determine a major gift is $1,000 and you currently have twenty donors giving at least that amount, you can hope to count on at least $20,000, or twenty donors, to launch the giving society. If you base your goal on giving potential as opposed to giving history, count one-third of donor prospects for your fundraising goal (you would want to ask three times the number of prospects to reach your goal).

    - Step 2: If you plan to invite each existing major donor to become founding members of the giving society and then ask each one to invite one friend, you can add $20,000 more to your goal, for a running total of $40,000.

    - Step 3: If you have a match incentive to join (refer to item 11 in this list), you can also encourage your donors who typically give around the $400 level to join with a $500 match. If you have twenty donors who give at this level, you can add $20,000 to your goal, for a running total of $60,000. (Note: You will need a donor or donors to commit $10,000 in matching funds to launch the giving society.)

3. **Articulate the need.** This is how you rally people toward a goal. Avoid restricting funds by using language like "Your gift will …" Share the need and what the funds mean to the mission. The giving society should support the organization's greatest needs (general operating). However, it is important to provide context to the value of the fundraising goal by sharing the impact the funds will have. For example, "Raising $300,000 could help us provide one million meals to people experiencing food insecurity."

4. **Research your donors.** Utilize a prospect-screening tool to research their giving capacity. The goal of a giving society is not only to get donors to join and provide support year after year but also to have them give more over time.

5. **Meet with your donors.** Ask for an in-person meeting to share the concept of a giving society and get their initial thoughts about participating in one. Ask if they would be part of a focus group to discuss the opportunity further.

6. **Conduct a focus group.** This group will help you identify a steering committee and founding members. It should be a nice lunch, ideally hosted at someone's home. The CEO should facilitate a discussion about the attributes of the giving society to get feedback and determine the interest in joining and supporting one.

7. **Name your society.** Ask for suggestions from your focus group and key stakeholders. Align the name with your mission. Consider creating a logo to give your giving society a brand and identity.

8. **Identify a chairperson.** If you are not able to readily identify a chairperson (or chairpersons), ask the focus group if they know anyone in their network who might be interested. Ask if they would be willing to connect you with that contact over breakfast or lunch. The chairperson must be willing to join the giving society with a leadership gift (the minimum giving level or more) as well as invite their friends to join. They must be passionate about the goal of the society. Determine what they need for inspiration to lead—stories, statistics, engagement opportunities, etc.

9. **Recruit a *steering committee*.** Ask your chairperson to help you recruit a steering committee to provide leadership and volunteer support for the giving society. The goal is to ensure that the society is peer led and not overly burdensome on a small organizational staff. Committee members are giving society members; they organize and host cultivation events and invite their friends to join the society. They underwrite events, manage membership, and implement other membership benefits.

   > **Committee members are giving society members; they organize and host cultivation events and invite their friends to join the society. They underwrite events, manage membership, and implement other membership benefits.**

10. **Provide a symbol of inclusion.** Give a bracelet, scarf, necklace, or other item that symbolizes your nonprofit and makes members feel special when they join.

11. **Provide a match incentive to join.** If it is $1,000 to join the giving society, offer a 1:1 match. This way, it would cost $500 to join the first year because a generous matching donor has provided the other $500.

12. **Ask people to join.** Consider asking new members to commit to a three-year pledge of participation. This will help you plan for its sustainability and growth. It also helps your organization plan for operating revenue. And to make it as easy as possible for people to join, consider giving members an option to pay their membership donation through automatic monthly payments.

13. **Plan cultivation events.** Fun cultivation events should be conducted quarterly. These are for society members to socialize and receive program updates. Additionally, they are opportunities for members to bring their friends to learn more about joining the society.

14. **Create a directory.** Provide a way for members to connect regularly. This can include a directory, a Facebook group, or other channels for communication.

15. **Promote membership.** A great way to promote membership in the giving society is to share society member testimonials and other stories of society impact in newsletters, on the website, and on social media.

16. **Provide an impact report.** Make sure that your members understand the impact of their giving as a group. The report should be formal. Consider a written impact report and an in-person celebration during which the CEO talks about the impact the society had over the past year.

GIVING DAYS

Giving Tuesday is the national version of a giving day. Many cities or regions also have local giving days that are supported by local funders. North Texas Giving Day, hosted by Communities Foundation of Texas (CFT), is held annually on the third Thursday of September. It brings in over $50 million from more than three thousand participating nonprofits. Through collaborative support by many community funders, nonprofits receive bonus funds and can secure cash prizes for participating in North Texas Giving Day.

We help our clients leverage a giving day with this advice:

1. **Incorporate giving days into your overall year-end fundraising strategy.** Be mindful about how these activities tie into your other year-end appeals or annual campaign so that you don't create donor fatigue. Consider using giving days as a kickoff to another call to action like joining a giving society.

2. **Develop a specific goal.** Achievable stretch goals drive success. During the giving day, follow progress toward your goal closely, and increase it if you can.

3. **Have a matching gift and promote it.** Since people love knowing their gift can make double the impact, promoting a match is a great way to get new donors!

4. **Get help.** Board and staff members should have outreach tasks as part of the agency's plan for giving days, building a culture of philanthropy and leveraging a larger network of contacts.

5. **Take advantage of free marketing opportunities and public events associated with local giving days.**

6. **Distinguish your agency with a unique communications strategy.** Consider more personalized approaches for previous or current donors.

7. **Follow the rules.** North Texas Giving Day, for example, requires that nonprofits not advise donors to give their outstanding pledges, such as event sponsorships, through giving days. Donations made through giving days are meant to be unrestricted gifts.

8. **Pay attention to hosted giving-day contests and special prize drawings.** Consider incorporating these into your giving-day communications plan.

9. **Have a plan to cultivate giving-day donors throughout the year.**

10. **Learn and adapt each year.** Talk through what worked and what didn't.

FRIENDS ASKING FRIENDS

This strategy, which found popularity through "a-thon" fundraising events, can now be implemented through an independent online giving platform, through a social media platform, or as an integral part of a giving-day strategy. Find success with these easy tips:

1. **Recruit others.** Participants create customized fundraising pages with a message about why they are asking friends to support the mission.

2. **Make it easy.** Provide participants with a tool kit that includes instructions, templates, and tips.

CHAPTER 9

3. **Make it direct.** "If everyone I sent this email to gives $10, I will hit my goal of $500." A direct ask allows them to make a quick decision on a "yes."

SMALL DONOR PARTIES

At these events, with usually fewer than fifty guests and hosted by a donor, friends and family learn more about a cause. This is a favorite strategy because it is a cost-effective, high-touch, and personal way to engage new donors and raise funds. For these parties, keep in mind:

1. **Host recruitment is key.** When recruiting hosts, prepare a one-page job description. The host should arrange and fund catering and expenses associated with the event. This person should also be a current major donor who is highly invested in your mission. Look at your board members to see who could fit into this role. When implementing this strategy for the first time, you may want to ask one or two highly engaged board members to help you test out the strategy and see how it could work on a larger scale. These individuals could then serve as peer influencers and advisors on future events.

2. **Be clear on purpose.** Ask the host to aim for a specific fundraising goal and to make the first gift, which would demonstrate their personal commitment to the mission.

3. **Determine setting.** The ideal setting is casual and intimate and in the donor's home, a small event space, or at the nonprofit.

4. **Invitations.** Guests should be invited personally by the host, with a minimum number of guests in mind. Provide the host with an invitation template.

5. **Introduce the organization.** Ideally, the host would introduce a representative from the organization to speak about the mission and services for no more than fifteen minutes, with about five minutes to respond to questions.

6. **The host makes the ask.** After explaining their own personal commitment to the mission, the host should then invite guests to get involved as donors, volunteers, or connectors. Have tools and resources on hand for immediate commitment. Follow up after the event.

7. **Make it easy for the host.** Provide a guide that includes instructions, templates, and scripts.

WISE PRO TIP: KNOW THE STATE LAWS ABOUT DONOR SOLICITATION

Did you know that nonprofits may be required to register as corporations in states where their donors reside? Every state has different requirements. Some require nonprofits to register, even if all they do is send solicitations or newsletters to, or receive online donations from, their residents. Tracking these requirements and states-of-origin of donations can be tedious. There are vendors that can handle this for you. Learn more through the Council of Nonprofits by going to councilofnonprofits.org.

PRIVATE FOUNDATIONS

As mentioned, grants can be game changers for nonprofits and provide catalytic funding for an organization. Let's take a look at some grant funder motivations and strategic considerations to inform your development plan.

Motivations

Most of the same motivations listed in the individual-giving section also apply to foundations. But there are differences. When developing cultivation strategies for foundations, consider the following:

- Many foundations have outlined on their websites giving guidelines that must be followed carefully. Not doing so can disqualify you.

- Most foundations are motivated by specific goals for impacting societal change or supporting people and communities they want to see flourish. It is important to have a strategy to cultivate each local foundation that has aligned with your mission. Call them to introduce your organization, invite them to events, and ask them to visit your programs. Attend funders forums and other events they attend or host.

- Most foundations make funding decisions based on a non-profit's demonstrated ability to meet a need or reach clearly defined goals (refer to chapter 1).

- Financial institutions are required to invest in low-income neighborhoods by the Community Reinvestment Act. If your programs involve affordable housing, workforce development, or financial skills, look to your local banks to determine their procedures for grant making. Many are moving to an invite-only process, so reach out and establish a connection.

- Foundation funders are often motivated by an organization or program's uniqueness. They want to know you are not dupli-cating services and are collaborating with nonprofits with similar programs or complementary services.

Giving Strategy

While chapter 3 provided an overview of grant writing as a strategy, here are some best practices for creating a grant-writing strategy for your development plan.

1. **Follow the Rule of Three Times.** At WISE, we create a grants plan that includes funder information and a potential ask amount for each grant application we plan to submit during the fiscal year. We segment the funding opportunities by the month we plan to work on the application—approximately one month prior to the deadline. If there's no deadline, put the funding opportunity in the plan about a year after the previous application or funding was received. Do not submit more than one application to a funder within a twelve-month period unless you are invited to. The ask amount is determined by the grant funder's typical grant size (refer to their IRS 990) and the size of your budget (remember, most funders will not fund over 25 percent of a budget). Your grants plan should have a total ask value that is a minimum of three times the grant revenue goal. If you do not have a history with grant writing, aim for four to five times your goal. Ask for more than you need, so that if you're given less, you might still hit your goal. Track your return rate so that in future years, you can build a plan based on these returns.

2. **Front-load your plan.** If you're implementing a grant-writing strategy for the first time, front-load your grants plan. Many family foundations do not have deadlines. Place all those funders at the beginning of your plan. Grants are a long-game strategy. You may wait six to twelve months or longer to hear back from a funder. Get applications out early

with the hopes you'll receive funding earlier in your fiscal year.

3. **Use a case for support.** At WISE, we write a general operating case for support and cover letter for each of our grant-writing clients. The case for support is a carefully crafted story demonstrating the case for funding. It should answer all key questions from a typical grant application. We do this for a couple of reasons. First, you should make the least restrictive ask whenever possible. Use the general operating case for support and cover letter as the proposal you send to those foundations with no specific application requirements. Second, while you do want to customize applications to appeal to the funder's interests, having a standard narrative about how you tell your story creates efficiency in your grant-writing strategy.

4. **Don't let capital be a cannibal.** If you are planning for a full-scale capital campaign or need to raise funds for a smaller capital needs project, be sure not to cannibalize from your sustainable operating or programmatic grant revenue. Ask your faithful foundation funders to consider giving above and beyond their typical grant in support of the capital project. On the flip side, don't waste an opportunity asking for a small grant from a funder who would give significantly more funding to a capital or growth strategy than they would to a general operating or program request. If there are funders in your plan that could make a large gift to a large project, save that ask for when you need it.

5. **Use a directory.** Foundation Center Directory and Grant-Station are helpful in sourcing foundation prospects. If you

cannot afford the subscriptions, check your local library, where you may be able to access foundation directories free of charge.

6. **Giving circles.** Get to know the giving circles or clubs in your community. These usually do not show up in the foundation directories. Get on their mailing lists, and make a note in your plan to look for the application when it is typically released.

CORPORATIONS

While many corporations have foundations and a formal grant-making process, there are many other ways they support their communities. With a larger corporation, you may be able to access support through the foundation philanthropic funds, marketing dollars for sponsorship opportunities, employee giving and volunteering, fundraising support (vendor campaigns), board or committee leadership, and pro bono skills.

Because companies are more likely to experience turnover with decision makers, the key to longevity is to build relationships with multiple leaders at different levels across the company.

Motivations

More than any other donor type, corporations are most likely to want a tangible return on investments. Corporate motivations are complex, and the best relationships are built upon a win-win framework. Consider the following motivations when approaching them:

- Corporations utilize marketing funds to sponsor fundraising events with a goal of receiving benefits like public recognition, access to their target market, and an opportunity to engage their employees and clients.

- Corporate foundations give philanthropic gifts to support specific giving interests that may align with their corporate mission or employee interests. Many corporate foundations are invite only. You will need to reach out and establish a relationship to receive an invitation to apply. Sometimes companies will get involved with a nonprofit in a small way, like through a volunteer project, and then evaluate the experience to determine whether they want to get more involved.

- Many companies will only financially support a nonprofit in which there is employee involvement. This may be in the form of board participation, employee volunteer projects, or employee advocation/nomination.

- Cobranding is also a strong motivator. For both the nonprofit and the company, cobranding has the benefit of alignment with a brand or mission, which can provide credibility to both parties.

Giving Strategies

Like individual giving, there are many more strategies for corporate giving than we have space for. But small nonprofits will find these corporate strategies to be particularly accessible and beneficial.

MATCHING GIFTS

Research to see if your donors work for companies that offer matching gifts. Some companies will provide a donation after an employee has volunteered a specific number of hours. Do not assume they will know about this employee benefit or that they will take care of the request for the match. I had a board member who kept forgetting to request matching funds for their donations, so I downloaded the form, filled it out, and brought it to the board meeting for him to sign.

PERSONAL VENDOR CAMPAIGNS

Don't forget that your board members and other volunteers have personal vendors—bankers, financial planners, insurance brokers, etc. Provide them with a script and email/letter template so that they can request a gift from their personal vendors to support your nonprofit. This works especially well when connected to a campaign.

FUNDRAISING EVENTS

While events appeal to corporations and individuals for sponsorship and other giving opportunities, they are ideal for corporate partners. For the purposes of preparing for your development plan, keep these things in mind:

1. **Create a reasonable financial plan.** When planning a fundraising event, create a detailed budget that includes the projected expenses and revenue breakdown by sponsorship level and other revenue sources. This should be created in conjunction with a pipeline of sponsor prospects. You should have a minimum of two prospects for every sponsorship you have added to the budget. If you have a fundraising goal to secure, say, five $10,000 sponsors, you should have ten prospects that you are approaching for a $10,000 sponsorship.

2. **Don't wait too long on a sponsor.** Make your presenting and other higher-level sponsor asks early (a year out from the event is ideal), and give them a deadline to decide, or make it clear there are other potential sponsors considering the same opportunity.

3. **Keep expenses reasonable.** This is worth repeating: when building the financial plan for your event budget, keep expenses at or below 25 percent.

WISE PRO TIP: DIRECT MARKETING TRIGGERS TAXES FOR YOUR NONPROFIT

One of my least favorite fundraising strategies is when nonprofits seek to benefit from a percentage of sales from a restaurant or other service provider. These are really marketing strategies for the restaurant and only make sense for organizations with a large built-in audience like schools. They often raise very little money and are a distraction for fundraisers.

Any marketing or sponsorship strategy that directly drives traffic to a business has the potential to trigger **unrelated business income tax (UBIT)**. UBIT is a tax on revenue generated from commercial activities outside the scope of your nonprofit's purpose. Avoid triggering it by not selling advertising space—remove the term "ad space" from your fundraising vocabulary. Also, avoid using language that is directive by nature. An example of this is by saying, "Coke is a proud sponsor of …" instead of "Drink Coke," or "Chipotle is pleased to support our school by donating 5 percent of every meal sold tonight to our school" instead of "Eat at Chipotle tonight, and 5 percent of your purchase will be donated back to our school." Another important UBIT-related rule is that if you are selling a product, the majority (85 percent minimum) has to be substantially performed and directed by volunteers (Girl Scout cookie sales, for example).

OTHER CORPORATE SPONSORSHIPS

Consider other events or activities that you can leverage for a sponsorship opportunity. Do you have workshops that companies can sponsor? How about community outreach efforts with volunteers who can wear T-shirts with corporate logos on them? Or perhaps you have a robust social media presence and audience that can be leveraged for a cobranding opportunity with a fun social media campaign.

WISE PRO TIP: CUSTOMIZE CORPORATE SPONSORSHIP PROPOSALS

Regarding corporate sponsorship proposals, provide your prospect with three possible levels of giving, based on the information you have gathered from meeting with them. One level should be what you think they will feel comfortable giving. The other two should be an option slightly above the first level and then one that will be a stretch. If you believe this prospective corporate donor is a $25,000 sponsor, you don't want to hand them a generic packet with giving ranges that start at $2,500. Follow this same customization for individual donors. An individual who donated $5,000 the previous year should not receive a letter asking for a $50 gift.

Understanding Key Elements of a Development Plan

Finally, armed with this information, you are ready to create a realistic development plan. You can download a template on our website.

Whether you use our template or another, it should include the following elements:

- Fundraising goals for each strategy

- A breakdown of how the fundraising goal will be achieved for each strategy

- Monthly or quarterly (at minimum) milestone goals

- A timeline of activities

- Major tactics for each fundraising strategy

- Costs associated with each fundraising strategy

- Needed resources like volunteers and in-kind support

- Person responsible for specific fundraising goals and activities

As you are building your plan, prioritize those strategies with the greatest potential return. If there is a strategy that has lower potential, but you don't want to scrap it completely, keep it as a gap strategy.

Gap strategies are supplemental strategies to implement when one of your primary strategies doesn't succeed. You can also develop a gap strategy by looking at ways you can increase revenue in your upcoming fundraising strategies. The important thing is that you use your milestone goals to assess progress and change direction as needed to reach your overall fundraising goal.

A WISE CASE STUDY: MAXIMIZING CAPACITY

During a fundraising assessment, we evaluate a client's existing capacity to determine whether there are ways to maximize it. Let's see what this looks like using the example of a recent client. They had the following fundraising results during their last fiscal year:

Annual giving day: $10,818 (this included a single $10,000 gift from a church)

Year-end giving appeal: $7,400

Open house donor event: $6,149

Golf tournament at Top Golf: $2,847

Gala: $8,570

Foundations: $82,219

Total fundraising revenue: $118,003

Our assessment led to a plan to more than double their revenue—not by adding new strategies but by maximizing the strategies they already have underway. Their fundraising results easily showed me that the golf tournament is likely a time waster because it doesn't have an appropriate return on the investment of resources. So I recommended the client drop this event and focus on growing other strategies, such as the small donor events. Subsequently, they increased the goal for their open house to $10,000 and also aimed to have five board members host these events, in which they'd introduce ten to twenty guests to the organization and ask them to donate. The total goal for the small donor event strategy was $60,000. We recommend this strategy often because it is a low-cost way to introduce new donors to the organization and build the individual donor base.

In this example, breaking down the goal into smaller chunks that can be owned by a handful of committed volunteers makes it more achievable and leverages the volunteer time more effectively than implementing a golf tournament. By maximizing existing capacity with an efficient strategy, we can turn roughly $9,000 of revenue that came from the golf and open house events into $60,000.

As we discussed in chapter 4, it is also important to ensure that you have entry points into the organization for different types of donors. This client had a promising grant-writing strategy with two volunteer grant writers, so we helped them create a plan to maximize their capacity by targeting funders with the greatest potential. By being strategic about which funders to apply to and rightsizing the ask amount, we developed a plan for a grants goal of $200,000.

We advised that they keep the gala as an entry point for corporate donors. It was produced on a small budget and well attended. By implementing a competitive sponsorship strategy and ticket price, we set a fundraising goal of $70,000.

The client had been a recipient of passive church giving and has an alignment with the Christian faith. They aimed to reach out to one church per month for a total of twelve and a fundraising goal of $30,000 ($2,500 per church). Each board member would be responsible to reach out to one church.

Finally, we maximized each individual-giving strategy using matching donors and reoccurring giving strategies. We didn't add any strategies, but we could show how implementing best practices could result in an increase of revenue. We set a fundraising goal for individual giving at $100,000.

If they achieved all these goals, they would double their revenue, allowing them to pay the executive director and hire program staff. For this to be doable:

- The plan must be followed without distraction. That means no competing fundraising activities.

- Effective people management is essential, communicating clear expectations with volunteers, then giving them the tools needed to be successful. For the open house parties and church strategies, a guide with step-by-step instructions, templates, and scripts will set up fundraising volunteers for success.

GOAL SETTING

When setting goals, there are a couple of strategies you can use:

Using Historical Data

If you have history with implementing a strategy, you can use historical information to set goals. The increase between last year's actuals and this year's goals can be established in several ways. You may elect to increase a goal by 5 to 15 percent. A percentage increase based on trends is the ideal way to increase the fundraising goal for grants.

You may also develop the pipeline of funding prospects first and then determine a reasonable goal from the prospects. If you have $1 million in total ask value in your grants plan, you could set your fundraising goal for this strategy at $330,000. For events, you could base your sponsorship goals on the number of solid prospects you have for each level.

You could also increase the goal for each tactic that supports the overall goal for a specific strategy. Let's say you have ten $5,000 sponsors for an event and a strong fundraising committee. Then you might want to add three $5,000 sponsors to the goal for that level. Increase each sponsorship level in a similar, modest fashion to lead to an overall reasonable increase in the event goal.

Starting from Scratch

If you are starting a new strategy, you can back into your fundraising goals. Perhaps you are developing a fundraising appeal to a two-hundred-member audience with an affinity toward your nonprofit. Then you could assume that the average gift per member will be $50. So $50 x 200 = $10,000.

Or you may have a prospect that could make a $20,000 challenge gift to motivate others to give on giving day. In that case, you could set a fundraising goal of $40,000.

For a board-giving strategy, you could assume $1,000 from each of your twenty board members for a total goal of $20,000.

The point of each example is that there is a clear breakdown of how you got to the goal, and it is based upon reasonable assumptions.

Now that you have a development plan, don't ignore it for the rest of the year. Your plan is a working document with milestone goals that let you know if you are on track toward success.

> **Now that you have a development plan, don't ignore it for the rest of the year. Your plan is a working document with milestone goals that let you know if you are on track toward success.**

Use Milestone Goals

It is essential that you build milestone goals into your development plan. These are short-term goals that lead to your long-term goals. Set quarterly goals at a minimum. Monthly goals are ideal. Often, organizations get close to the end of their fiscal year before they realize that they have no chance of reaching the goals outlined in the development plan. Make the plan work for you—treat it as your road map.

Word to the WISE

Download the development plan template from the website. Schedule your brainstorming session, and get started creating your realistic development plan for the year.

CONCLUSION

Acts of sacrifice and decency without regard to what's in it for you create a ripple effect. Ones that lift up families and communities, that spread opportunity.
—BARACK OBAMA

Thank you for taking the time to read *Become a Nonprofit Pro*. As a fellow changemaker, you picked up this book with the hope of taking your time, talents, and treasure to new levels of meaningful impact. I hope you found what you were looking for and that you continue to create ripple effects that transform entire communities.

Don't forget to visit www.wiseresourcedevelopment.com to download supplemental tools and tips to support your organization.

GLOSSARY OF TERMS

Affiliate: An organization directly or indirectly controlled by, or under common control of, another organization. For nonprofit organizations, this refers to the local office of a national nonprofit. It is also commonly referred to as a chapter.

Asset-based language: The intentional shift to narratives that define communities by their "aspirations and contributions," rather than any potential challenges or deficits.

Attestation: The act of bearing witness to a document's authenticity by signing one's name to it to affirm that it is genuine.

Angel donor: Individual who makes investments very early into the formation of a new nonprofit, usually as a result of believing in the founder's vision.

Balance sheet: A financial statement that reports an organization's assets and liabilities at a specific point in time.

Benchmark: A tool used to determine how well an organization is performing relative to its peers to identify best practices and opportunities and subsequently to adapt and improve.

Board matrix: A tool that helps an organization review and assess the expertise, connections, lived experiences, and leadership capacity of current and prospective board members.

Brand: How an organization communicates its purpose. It influences how others see the organization and its mission and can include visual, narrative, and behavioral aspects of the organization.

Breach of duty: The failure to perform a promised act or obligation.

Capital: In nonprofits, capital is often used to refer to tangible or physical needs like a building, furniture, or technology.

Capital campaign: A targeted fundraising effort that takes place over a defined period of time to raise funds for a tangible purpose, usually a building or renovation.

Certified public accountant (CPA): An officially accredited member of the accounting profession.

Charter: A legal document that sets up the structure of the organization, outlining the processes by which rules are made and enforced. For national organizations, local affiliates may have a charter that associates them as a member of the national organization.

Chief development officer: An executive-level employee at a nonprofit who holds duties such as overseeing the financial stability, fundraising, or growth of the organization.

Chief programs officer: An executive-level individual responsible for managing the day-to-day operations of a company's programs. They oversee all aspects of these programs, including planning, implementation, and evaluation.

Collateral materials: Print materials that promote an organization and its activities.

Community impact: To have a direct effect on the community.

Community need: The gap between what services currently exist in a community and what should exist.

Compliance: Conformity in fulfilling official requirements.

Constituent relationship management (CRM) system: A dynamic database that tracks and manages an organization's interactions with its constituents.

Contributed revenue: Gifts made freely without receiving any goods or services in exchange. These include donations, grants, and noncash donations. Usually used to refer to charitable donations that are not restricted to a purpose like government grants or contracts.

Control mechanisms: A system used to keep one or more variable parameters constant, or within specified bounds.

Corporate solicitation: Requesting money on behalf of charitable organizations from corporations in the form of sponsorship.

Culture of philanthropy: A subset of organizational culture or how its members interact and behave that emphasizes the belief in philanthropy—voluntary action for the common good.

Data management system: A computerized data-keeping system that collects, stores, and protects an organization's data so it can be analyzed for organizational decisions.

Deficit: This occurs when an organization does not meet the spending, fundraising, or budget goal.

Deduping: An abbreviation for "deduplication." Optimizing data storage by eliminating duplicate copies of data.

Demographics: The statistical characteristics of human populations (such as age or income) used especially to identify markets.

Development: A component of a comprehensive advancement team; reflects proactive work to develop a wide range of resources for the organization.

Development committee: A committee composed of individuals with influence and connectivity within the community who focus on building new relationships for the organization capable of making significant philanthropic investments.

Development director: An individual who oversees all of an organization's fundraising activities. The development director is typically the senior fundraiser for the organization. Depending on the title structure of the organization, this position may be titled chief development officer or vice president of development.

Development plan: The strategic measurable fundraising goals that an organization plans to meet within a certain amount of time.

Diversity, equity, inclusion, and accessibility (DEIA): A way of thinking about what constitutes a model workplace and an effort to lean into the human-centric nature of nonprofits. It is a way to fully realize the abilities and contributions of all individuals.

- Diversity: The practice of including many communities, identities, races, ethnicities, backgrounds, abilities, cultures, and beliefs.

- Equity: The consistent and systematic, fair, just, and impartial treatment of all individuals.

- Inclusion: The recognition, appreciation, and use of the talents and skills of people of all backgrounds.

- Accessibility: The design, construction, development, and maintenance of facilities, information and communication technology, programs, and services so that all people, including people with disabilities, can fully and independently use them.

Donor base: Everyone who has given donations to a nonprofit.

Donor Bill of Rights: Rights created by the Association of Fundraising Professionals (AFP), the Association for Healthcare Philanthropy (AHP), the Council for Advancement and Support of Education (CASE), and the Giving Institute: Leading Consultants to Nonprofits. Used to ensure that philanthropy merits the respect and trust of the general public and that donors and prospective donors can have full confidence in the not-for-profit organizations and causes they are asked to support. The bill includes the following rights:

1. To be informed of the organization's mission, of the way the organization intends to use donated resources, and of its capacity to use donations effectively for their intended purposes.

2. To be informed of the identity of those serving on the organization's governing board and to expect the board to exercise prudent judgment in its stewardship responsibilities.

3. To have access to the organization's most recent financial statements.

4. To be assured their gifts will be used for the purposes for which they were given.

5. To receive appropriate acknowledgment and recognition.

6. To be assured that information about their donation is handled with respect and with confidentiality to the extent provided by law.

7. To expect that all relationships with individuals representing organizations of interest to the donor will be professional in nature.

8. To be informed whether those seeking donations are volunteers, employees of the organization, or hired solicitors.

9. To have the opportunity for their names to be deleted from mailing lists that an organization may intend to share.

10. To feel free to ask questions when making a donation and to receive prompt, truthful, and forthright answers.

Donor database: Software system that nonprofits use to securely store and manage donor information, segment the data, pull reports, and monitor other key performance indicators (KPIs). This information includes everything from their contact information and giving history to their interests and past involvement with the organization.

Donor fatigue: A lessening of a donor's willingness to respond generously to charitable appeals, resulting from the frequency of such appeals.

Endowment: Assets (usually cash accounts that are invested in equities or bonds, or other investment vehicles) set aside so that the original assets grow over time as a result of income earned from interest on the underlying invested funds. For nonprofits, endowments provide a sustainable source of revenue.

Event committee: A committee of volunteers committed to the success of a fundraising event with implementation and fundraising responsibilities.

Event manager: An individual who oversees the process of planning and implementing events for a nonprofit. As a best practice, this position should have a fundraising performance goal attached to the events they manage.

Evidence-based best practices: The objective, balanced, and responsible use of current research and the best available data to guide practice decisions, such that outcomes are improved.

Executive director: The senior operating officer or manager of an organization, usually at a nonprofit. Sometimes referred to as a chief executive officer (CEO). Their duties are similar to those of a for-profit company CEO: Responsible for strategic planning, working with the board of directors, and operating within a budget.

Executive team: The topmost level of organizational leadership that comprises of a group of people who are responsible for setting strategic goals and planning, directing, and coordinating the activities of the organization.

Feasibility study: The assessment of the practicality of a proposed project or plan.

Financial audit: An objective examination and evaluation of an organization's financial statements conducted by a certified public accountant to make sure that the financial records are a fair and accurate representation of the transactions they claim to represent.

Financial compilation report: A report prepared by the accountant that accompanies the compiled financial statements.

Financial malfeasance: An act that causes intentional damage and involves the management of an organization's financials in a way that deliberately hides the financial reality.

Financial management software: A tool that helps an organization manage and govern income, expenses, and assets.

Financial systems: The tools and processes that help a nonprofit effectively manage its financials.

Financial statement review: A service under which the accountant obtains limited assurance that there are no material modifications that need to be made to an entity's financials to be in conformity with GAAP standards.

Financial transparency: Processes and practices of providing potential donors with a clear understanding of the financial well-being of the organization.

Fiscally responsible: The act of creating, optimizing, and maintaining a balanced budget and financially sustainable organization.

Fiscal year: The year used for accounting and tax purposes. May be different from a calendar year.

Fundraising: The organized activity of raising funds (for an institution or political cause).

Fundraising assessment: An audit of the organization's fundraising efforts that is performed by a third party or outside consultant. Consists of evaluating current fundraising strategies and methods, identifying strengths and opportunities for improvement, and providing feedback on where and how to improve.

Generally Accepted Accounting Principles (GAAP): A common set of accounting rules, standards, and procedures issued by the

Financial Accounting Standards Board (FASB). Consult a certified public accountant for more information.

Gap strategy: A fundraising strategy that is implemented when the original strategy has not achieved its fundraising goal.

General operating expense: An expense that an organization incurs through its normal operations, including rent, equipment, marketing, payroll, insurance, etc. Sometimes "operating expenses" and "administrative expenses" are terms used interchangeably.

Give-get policy: A requirement that all directors on the organization's board "give" and "get" financial resources for the organization.

Giving strategy: The way in which donors achieve their giving goals. A successful fundraising strategy will provide easy and responsive opportunities for donors to meet their giving goals with the nonprofit.

Grant funders: Institutions (usually government agencies or foundations) that provide funding for a program, service, or activity.

Grant writing: A fundraising strategy that helps organizations secure grant funding for projects, services, or goods.

In-kind donation: A nonmonetary gift given to a nonprofit, including goods, services, use of equipment or facilities, and labor.

Institutional donor: A grant-making entity. The most common institutional donors are government agencies and private foundations.

Internal controls: Accounting and auditing processes used in an organization's finance department that ensure the integrity of financial reporting and regulatory compliance.

IRS Form 990: The formal title is "Return of Organization Exempt from Income Tax." It is a US Internal Revenue Service form that provides the public with a nonprofit organization's financial information, such as income, expenses, and activities during the past year.

Job Description: Informative documentation of the scope, duties, tasks, responsibilities, and working conditions related to the job listing in the organization through the process of job analysis. Also details the skills and qualifications that an individual applying for the job needs to possess.

Key performance indicator (KPI): A quantifiable measurement to evaluate success.

Logic model: A visual representation of the organization's planned programming or a road map of how the organization intends to achieve the desired outcomes using defined resources and strategies.

Limited assurance: When the CPA performs enough work to indicate they are not aware of any inconsistencies in the accounting system.

Major gifts solicitation: The act of presenting an opportunity for someone to share significant material assets, resulting in an intangible reward and sense of fulfillment for the donor and a significant difference for the organization.

Management letter: A formal communication from the auditor to the organization intended to provide those charged with governance with valuable information regarding the organization's financial position or systems that need to be corrected.

Material modifications: Changes made to financial statements to be in accordance with GAAP standards.

Mission creep: An unplanned or unofficial shift in organizational goals.

Money chasing: Pursuing or accepting funds for a project or initiative that doesn't align with the organization's mission.

Operations: Procedures and systems used to carry out the organization's day-to-day activities.

Organizational chart: A tool that provides a graphic representation of the staff roles, responsibilities, relationships between members, and hierarchical ranks of a nonprofit's members.

Organizational life cycle: The process by which organizations grow and decline through changes in systems and processes that support the organization's existence.

Organizational readiness: The extent to which organizational members are psychologically and behaviorally prepared to implement organizational change.

Outcome measure: A metric that demonstrates how much better off the organization's clients, or society, are because of a nonprofit's activities and programming.

Outcome measurement: A systematic way to assess the extent to which a program has achieved its intended results.

Performance management: The process of maintaining or improving employee job performance using performance assessment tools and coaching.

Philanthropic dollars: Donations of money from an individual or organization that are used to support a cause.

Profit and loss statement: A financial statement that summarizes the revenue, costs, and expenses incurred during a specified period, usually a quarter or fiscal year.

Project plan: A document referred to during the execution of a particular project to ensure that it will be completed efficiently and effectively within a specified time frame. It usually includes a breakdown of tasks, deadlines, and persons responsible.

Prospect: Individual or organization that a nonprofit will cultivate or is cultivating to become a donor; includes current donors identified as potential donors for a specific project or campaign.

Prospect scoring: Scores assigned to prospects based on their engagement with an organization and public information about assets and philanthropic involvement.

Quality controls: A system of maintaining standards.

Reimbursement grants: Funding to grant recipients after expenses have been incurred.

Resource: A useful or valuable possession or quality that a person or organization has—for example, money, time, or skills.

Restricted funds: A donation that has been earmarked for specific or limited purpose by the donor.

Request for proposals (RFP): A document that announces a project, describes it, and solicits bids from qualified contractors to complete it.

Return on investment (ROI): A ratio that compares the gain or loss from an investment relative to its costs.

Revenue projection: An estimate of how much money an organization will generate over a set period of time.

Risk management: The process of identifying, assessing, and controlling financial, legal, strategic, and security risks to an organization.

Scenario planning: Planning that enables nonprofit leaders to prepare for potential challenges or opportunities and to be ready to respond quickly and appropriately. It asks nonprofit leaders to consider factors partially or entirely outside of the organization's control, how those factors might shift, and how the organization could respond.

Segment donors: The process of breaking donors into categories based on shared characteristics, such as age, donation history or geographical area.

Single audit: An examination of an organization that spends at least $750,000 of federal grants and awards per year. It is intended to provide assurance to the government that its funds are being expended appropriately and that the targeted entity has adequate internal financial controls in place.

SMART (Specific, Measurable, Achievable, Realistic, and Timebound): The way that the goal is expressed should target the issue precisely (specific), be translated into some measurable form (measurable), and be set in a way that provides the best possible outcome for the provider (achievable), yet is within the provider's capabilities (realistic). It is also important to be clear about when the objective will be achieved (timebound).

Social capital: The value or resources that people and groups get from their networks and relationships.

Solicit: Any request of contributions or gifts made in written or verbal form or by television, radio, or telephone.

Special event: A social engagement that brings together people from the organization and community to raise funds for a cause. For nonprofit organizations, some of the common types of events include runs/walks, gala dinners, and golf tournaments.

Steering committee: A committee of volunteers that leads a project.

Stewardship: The relationship-building and communications that take place between a donor and an organization after the gift has been received.

Strategic: The way in which an organization decides what it wants to achieve and plans actions and use of resources over time to do this.

Subclasses: A secondary or subordinate class. In accounting, these help with greater detail and tracking of financial expenditures.

Sustainable: A nonprofit's ability to sustain itself over the long term, perpetuating its ability to fulfill its mission. Includes the concepts of financial sustainability, as well as leadership succession planning, adaptability, and strategic planning.

SWOT (Strengths, Weaknesses, Opportunities, and Threats) analysis: A technique for assessing the performance, competition, risk, and potential of an organization and to develop strategic planning.

- Strengths: What an organization excels at and what differentiates it from others.

- Weaknesses: Factors that stop an organization from performing at its optimum level. These are areas where the business needs to improve.

- Opportunities: Favorable external factors that give an organization a competitive advantage.

- Threats: Factors that have the potential to harm an organization.

Thought leader: A person whose views are taken to be authoritative and influential.

Unconscious bias: The unconscious favoritism toward or prejudice against people of a particular ethnicity, gender, or social group that influences one's actions or perceptions.

Unrelated business income: Income from activities that are not substantially related to the purposes for which the nonprofit's tax-exempt status was recognized.

Unrelated business income tax (UBIT): A tax that is imposed on the unrelated business income generated by tax-exempt organizations.

Unrestricted revenue: Grants or donations can be spent in any way the organization believes is appropriate to further its mission.

Value proposition: A service or feature that makes an organization unique and attractive to constituents.

Volunteer: The act of contributing free labor to conduct community service or support a nonprofit organization.

White saviorism: The belief that white people are here to save, help, teach, and protect their nonwhite counterparts.

Whistleblower policy: A core policy for nonprofits that encourages volunteers and employees to communicate their concerns about most any issue without fear of retaliation.

ABOUT TAWNIA WISE

Tawnia Wise blazes the trail for nonprofits in need of capacity and resources to support their mission. Harnessing over a decade of experience in leadership roles at notable organizations including Volunteers of America Texas, Baylor Scott & White–Irving Foundation, Mothers Against Drunk Driving, the American Heart Association, and the Cystic Fibrosis Foundation, she founded Wise Resource Development (WISE) in 2014 to broaden her ability to impact the nonprofit sector. Since the beginning, clients have turned to Tawnia for her wise counsel and her focus on getting results. Under her leadership as founder and CEO, WISE has grown into one of the most sought-after nonprofit consultancies in Dallas–Fort Worth and beyond. With a goal of transforming nonprofit consulting, WISE combines strategy and tactical support to help clients of all sizes elevate their organization's ability to serve their mission. She is passionate about mission work that focuses on poverty, social justice, mental health, reentry services, and youth from hard places. Tawnia has a master's in public administration and is a certified fundraising executive. She lives in Carrollton, Texas, and is the proud mother of Cole and Carmyn.

Connect with Tawnia Wise on social media, or at www.tawniawise.com or www.wiseresourcedevelopment.com.

Printed in the USA
CPSIA information can be obtained
at www.ICGtesting.com
JSHW021522110324
58997JS00004B/192